THE MIND-BODY-SPIRIT MENTOR

Seven Simple Steps to Upscale
Your Mastery of Money, Relationships and Health

Anne Corbin

The Mind-Body-Spirit Mentor: Seven Simple Steps to Upscale Your Mastery of Money, Relationships and Health
www.TheMind-Body-SpiritMentor.com
Copyright © 2022 ANNE CORBIN

ISBN: 979-8-404553-60-4

Limits of Liability and Disclaimer of Warranty
The author and publisher shall not be liable for your misuse of the enclosed material. This book is strictly for informational and educational purposes only.

Warning – Disclaimer
The purpose of this book is to educate and entertain. The author and/or publisher do not guarantee that anyone following these techniques, suggestions, tips, ideas, or strategies will become successful. The author and/or publisher shall have neither liability nor responsibility to anyone with respect to any loss or damage caused, or alleged to be caused, directly or indirectly by the information contained in this book.

Published by
10-10-10 Publishing
200-455 Apple Creek Blvd
Markham ON Canada

First 10-10-10 Publishing paperback edition January 2022

CONTENTS

Also by Anne Corbin

Property Investing 2020 and Beyond
The Authorities : Everything is Energy

"You can't connect the dots looking forward; you can only connect them looking backwards. So you have to trust that the dots will somehow connect in your future. You have to trust in something – your gut, destiny, life, karma, whatever. Because believing that the dots will connect down the road will give you the confidence to follow your heart even when it leads you off the well-worn path; and that will make all the difference."

Steve Jobs [Stanford commencement address, June 2005]

For Marjorie, John and Mark, with gratitude and love.

Foreword

Have you been working on your personal development and setting goals according to the usual instructions, but find that you are suffering those well-known feelings of disappointment, frustration and maybe even despondency when results remain stubbornly unwilling to manifest for you? Maybe you have the sense that there must be a missing link, a certain key with which to unlock that famous Law of Attraction and make it work for you. If so, then this book is an absolute must read.

Anne Corbin has been interested in energy medicine for many years but she was too busy to devote serious study time and investigation into what is an incredible revelation, but which represents information that may be unknown to you. Anne writes with obvious conviction and enthusiasm for her subject, explaining just why this knowledge has remained essentially underground, withheld or considered beyond your reach.

Anne's easy-to-read style is a reflection of her personality – open and down to earth, with flashes of wit and humour. She writes from the heart, and there is much valuable wisdom and experience contained within the pages of this book.

If you imagined that the ability to heal was a gift bestowed only on a select few, think again! Your body was designed to repair itself, and self-healing is a skill available to you. The idea that you need to reach for chemical remedies for everyday ailments is fundamentally flawed. You will find this book highly informative, and very engaging, as Anne addresses aspects of health and holistic living that might be completely new to you.

Anne is a qualified maths and science teacher, and also a chartered accountant with 20 years' experience in practice and in business. She combines her broad practical knowledge of science with her first love, education, as she develops her argument and shows you a framework on which you can build a new way of life.

You will gain a surprising and unexpected insight into the worlds of holistic health, spirituality and personal development, all of which are areas of profound interest to Anne. As she shares her knowledge with you, her highest values of growth and education will inspire you to add to your own learning, recognize numerous unexplored possibilities, and develop your full potential.

I highly recommend this book, and hope that you will find it as worthwhile as I have. You could discover that it points you in a whole new direction, towards new goals, new fulfilment and new purpose in your life. It will certainly change your perspective and no doubt will inspire you to explore different ideas and lesser travelled pathways.

Danielle Coppolaro
National Vice President, Arbonne International

Acknowledgements

Firstly, I want to thank my parents: Marjorie, whose warmth, vision and generosity set me up for life; and John, whose sharp intellect, calm nature and practical approach provided memorable balance right from the earliest years. I thank my brother, Mark, for his unfailing support and for his brilliant sense of humour. Also, my late husband, Roger, who might be watching my progress with interest from another plane.

In addition, thanks to my "surrogate parents," Pat and Patsy Patient, who made me one of the family when I was living far from home in Halls at University. Also, to Lorna and David Seymour Cousins and to my great long-standing friends, Cliff and Gill Paget, Rod and Jenny Shaw, Gabriella La Commare and Mike Hackett, and Jacqui McCloy. Special thanks to Roger Farge from Bermuda for re-introducing excitement into my life, and sharing some of the best times. Plus, of course, all my many, many new friends in the world of property.

I thank my many teachers and lecturers; in particular, Mrs Howard, Mrs Thompson and Mrs Morgan, Prof Ricketts and Prof Shaw. I recognise the valuable trainings of the many speakers and mentors whose views and visions are so readily available, thanks to modern technology; and I mention in particular, David Snyder, Alan Watts, David Icke, Simon Sinek, John Lamb Lash, Tony Robbins, David Wilcock and Dr Joe Dispenza.

I value examples set by many historical and political figures and would mention in particular, Winston Churchill, Cecil Rhodes, Margaret Thatcher and Ian Douglas Smith. I recognise Andrew Wakefield, Mordechai Vanunu and David Kelly, who were crushed by the System for speaking the truth.

I thank all the wonderful authors who have inspired me over the years and implanted an undying love of reading. I mention Boris Pasternak, David Yallop, Margaret Mitchell, Alexander Kent, Frederick Forsyth, Neville Shute, Anthony Horowitz and Ken Follett, but the list could include hundreds of names. In particular, I credit the great Enid Blyton for getting me started in the first place.

In recent years, I have turned my attention more towards non-fiction and discovered the writings of Napoleon Hill, Robert Cialdini, Neale Donald Walsch, Maxwell Maltz, Jose Silva, Ian Wilson and many others. I am grateful for their insights and teachings and for opening up a new world of possibilities.

Finally, I express gratitude to my trainers and mentors, past and present. In particular, I value guidance from Rob Moore, Mark Homer, Paul and Aniko Smith, Ray McLennan, Raymond Aaron, Paul O'Mahoney, David Cavanagh and Dr Sue Morter.

Chapter 1

Wisdom from the East

"Modern psychology has pointed to the need for educating people to use a much larger portion of the mind. Transcendental meditation fulfils this need."
Maharishi Mahesh Yogi

Masters and Mentors

If you had been one of the congregation attending the funeral of **Steve Jobs**, you would have received, as his parting gift, a book that he had described as his all-time favourite. He had been so deeply impressed by the subject matter that he wanted to participate in passing on the wisdom and teachings of the writer, **Paramahansa Yogananda.**

Steve Jobs died in 2011, having lost his final battle with pancreatic cancer. He was the co-founder and CEO of Apple, and was from the start an inspirational speaker, even in the early years of his profession. His short and motivational Stanford Commencement Address can be found on YouTube, and at the time of writing, this had over 40 million views.

The book by **Paramahansa Yogananda** is *Autobiography of a Yogi,* and when I learnt about the parting gift story, I immediately went out and bought a copy. It wasn't the sort of book I would ever have chosen myself, having never heard of the author, who died in 1952. He had been a Hindu master, or saint, and was responsible for introducing yoga to America and the West.

Up until then, I had only the vaguest concept of Hinduism. I had visited Kerala, in South-West India, and seen the very ornate temples for which this religion is famous. The temples are very brightly decorated, with numerous statues representing hundreds of deities. I was also aware of a few of the more famous amongst these: Vishnu, Kali, Saraswati, Lakshmi and Brahma. But that was all. And there was the revered Gandhi, whose life story was made famous in the award-winning film by **Richard Attenborough** (1982).

Autobiography of a Yogi endowed me with a new respect for the religious practices of Hinduism, and a determination to learn just a little more about each of the major religions of the world.

At this point, I should declare that although I was raised a Catholic, I can't profess to be one anymore, as I do not comply with the requisite rules and regulations. I am still Christian at heart, but dare I say that as I've grown older and learnt more, I find spirituality a far more appealing pursuit. This is a huge and important distinction, so much so that I have devoted the whole of Chapter 2 to the debate. Spirituality is something which has been allocated much higher importance in Eastern traditions, and this is why meditation plays such a large part in the lives of all, from childhood.

Within Christianity, there are numerous Saints, many of whom have died for their faith, and are known as martyrs, but the official requirement for sainthood is to be acknowledged as responsible for at least two miracles. (The late Pope John Paul II was rapidly declared a saint, after his death in 2005, although at the time, only one miracle had been proven. Presumably, an exception can be made for Popes!)

Catholicism doesn't ban interest in other religions, but it conveys the impression that they are invariably misguided, that followers are on the wrong path and (in the past, at least) that entry to heaven will be denied to them. Even as a young child, I considered this not only unfair but ridiculous. However, it was pointless to argue, and when I tried it at school, several teachers became extremely annoyed and floundered as they failed to convince me.

Hinduism and other Eastern religions also recognise thousands of saints, not only deceased but also while living. India is renowned as a particularly holy country and could possibly be where the first religion originated. Traditionally, serious students there are trained one-on-one by masters, also known as gurus. Jesus is recognised as a master in most of these religions, and is greatly respected. The author, then known as **Mukanda,** was trained as a monk by his guru, **Sri Yukteshwa.** When the master deemed that he was ready, the title of Swami was bestowed upon him and he chose the new name **Yogananda**. Paramahansa came many years later and was an acknowledgement of his achievement in spreading the word in the USA. **Paramahansa Yogananda** was a master and a saint, and at the time of his burial, 21 days after his death, there was absolutely no sign of decay on his body.

The Missing 18 Years

Yeshua Ben Joseph was born in a stable in Bethlehem just over 2000 years ago, according to the Bible. He was Jewish, spoke Aramaic and is the central figure in the New Testament.

The story of his birth is told in the Gospels, along with a few incidents up to the age of 12, after which there is a mysterious silence, until he appears again when John the Baptist was being hailed by some as the long awaited Messiah. The Jews had been longing for the prophesied messiah for thousands of years, and John was apparently arousing considerable interest as a candidate for the position.

The Hebrew word "messiah" translates into Greek as "christos," and into English as "the anointed one."

Jesus's public life lasts only 3 years, but during that time, he performed miracles, taught a very strong message—frequently in the form of parables or stories—and attracted a huge following, to the great concern of the religious leaders of the time, the Pharisees and Sadducees of the Sanhedrin. They perceived him as a threat, and accused him of blasphemy. The Gospels recount the story of how these men conspired with the Roman occupiers of Judea to have Jesus removed, involving the shameful and public execution by crucifixion.

Far from being silenced, Jesus rose from the dead—the ultimate miracle—an event celebrated by Christians every year at Easter. The early Christian movement grew slowly, as people at the time were largely illiterate, and so information was generally spread by word of mouth. Even the Gospels were written down many years after Jesus's death, which was at the age of 33.

What happened to him during the years between ages 12 and 30? Let us suppose Jesus was absent from the region during those 18 years. This would explain why there was no local knowledge of his activity. We know from the Bible account of his first miracle, that when his mother asked him to do something about the lack of wine, at the wedding feast of Cana, Jesus said, "Woman, my hour is not yet come." It makes sense that Jesus might have removed himself from the area, returning only when he was ready to begin in his short but predestined public life.

In 1894, a Russian traveller, **Nicolas Notovitch,** published a book in French, called *The Life of Saint Issa*, which claims that Jesus spent 17 years in India and Tibet where he learned Sanskrit, the Vedas and the Buddhist Canon. The Russian had spent six weeks recuperating in the Hemis Monastery in Ladakh, having broken his leg in a fall. During that time, the head Lama had read to him from documents relating these facts. English scholars at the time condemned the idea absolutely, labelled the book as a hoax, and **Notovitch** was utterly discredited. A British official even travelled to the monastery to make enquiries, but the monks—not surprisingly given the politics of the time—denied all knowledge of their visitor.

In 1922, **Swami Vivikananda** visited the monastery, and although his intention had been to discredit the Saint Issa story once and for all, he was amazed to learn that indeed a Russian had stayed there, for 6 weeks with a broken leg, and was able to see and translate some of the ancient manuscript for himself.

The film *Jesus in India* was released in 2008, but was not well received despite contributions from respected professors, the **Dalai Lama** and a papal nuncio. Personally, I became aware of it only very recently when researching St Issa. Does the general lack of reaction to comparatively recent publicity, in this, the Information Age, speak to the indifference felt by so many in the West about Christianity? It seems to me that in the late nineteenth century, when staunch Christianity was the norm in Europe and the West, **Notovitch's** book created much more interest—indeed controversy and outrage.

St Issa appears in the Muslim and Hindu world, and Buddhists refer to an ancient manuscript kept in a monastery in the Himalayas. **Paramahansa Yogananda** suggests that at least one of the Magi (the Wise Men of the Nativity story) was from India and that therefore it is more than likely that an inclination to visit India had been imbued into the holy child. It is thought that Jesus spent around ten years in Tibet and seven in Puri, northern India. It would not have been too difficult for Jesus to undertake the necessary travel, as the silk routes were well used and it would only have been a requirement for him to join one of the many caravans. Jesus would have been able to have completed his education and have received in-depth training from Eastern masters, enabling him to return to his homeland saturated with very unusual and esoteric knowledge.

More Lives Than One

Reincarnation is another of those beliefs long accepted in the East but not generally embraced in the West. It goes hand in hand with the teaching of karma or atonement. If you do not neutralise your bad deeds by the time you die, the obligation to do so will still be with you in your next life. The concept is that, as spirits, we experience many lives, using different bodies. Old souls are those who have lived multiple times, keep coming back for more and have developed a deep wisdom. Young souls tend not to find such arcane subjects interesting and are happy to be part of the herd, follow instruction and do what they are told without questioning it.

When I began to research reincarnation, I discovered that it had been a pillar of belief amongst the early Christians. All references to reincarnation were removed from the Bible at the Council of Nicaea in AD325. By this time, the Roman emperor Constantine had converted to Christianity and made the political decision that it should become the religion of the Roman Empire, having recognised the unifying power of a common creed.

Constantine's seal of approval followed actions by others in the previous century, who had attempted to mould the new religion, incorporating certain practices belonging to numerous existing religions and dismissing others. In AD553, reincarnation was finally and officially condemned.

Regardless of which authority deleted practically all references to reincarnation from the Christian scriptures, the removal has deprived millions of a very practical and logical framework. It helps make sense of all sorts of unfairness in this world: Why are some born to a life of ease, wealth or happiness when others eke out a living below the poverty line, living in constant fear of floods, famine or other disasters? All this from a just and loving God? Very hard to explain when you are under the impression that you only get one shot at this life. And if one believed that any and all evil deeds committed would have to be paid for in a future life if not the present one, would that not moderate bad behaviour?

For Christians who affirm that if it's not in the Bible, it's outside of what constitutes the Word of God, there are numerous verses that take on a new meaning when viewed from a different perspective. Considering this statement in connection with reincarnation, references obviously are hard to find, with all overt mentions of reincarnation having been removed, and there is an enormous amount to scrutinise. However, in Luke, Mark and Matthew, there are references to John the Baptist being Elijah, returned to life. Also in Matthew, who tells the parable of the man born blind whose sight was restored by Jesus, the disciples ask whether the man was responsible for his own blindness, or whether it was the sin of his parents. How could he be responsible himself, unless he had lived a previous life?

In fairness, the Bible is quite hard to read anyway, even though much of the language in the King James Version is poetic and beautiful. Not only is it presented in seventeenth century English, much of it reads as if it was written in code. Indeed, this was probably the case, because at the time of the original writing, the authors were operating in an environment of secrecy and fear. The text will have been translated at least twice, from the original to Greek and then to English. In 1952, the latest Revised Standard Version (RSV) was produced—there were earlier RSVs in 1885 and 1901. Supposedly, these texts would be easier to digest and understand—but still more might have been "lost in translation."

This is an interesting and blatant mistranslation: When Jesus was dying on the cross, right at the end, he cried out: "Eli, Eli, Lama Sabachthani," which is traditionally taught as, "My God, my God, why hast thou forsaken me?" A more accurate translation, apparently, is "My God, my Sun, thou hast poured thy radiance upon me!" thus turning a cry of desperation into a statement of triumph, because it refers to Pagan initiation rites, successfully completed! The intentional mistranslation goes right back to the first translation into Greek, according to **Ralston Skinner,** in *The Hebrew Egyptian Mystery in the Source of Measures.*

Remember, Remember

If we identify our true "self" as a spirit, rather than a body, this idea sits particularly well with reincarnation. However, we might wonder why no memory exists for us of our previous lives.

It appears that a very few actually have such recollections. I personally am acquainted with certain individuals with memories of being in the womb, newly born, and of the birth process itself. Probably most of us are quite comfortable without such memories! But indeed, there's a vast difference in memory capacities with respect even to our lives on Earth. When does memory really begin? And how clear is anyone's memory from many years previously? For most of us, studies have shown memory starts around age 30 to 36 months. What details do we record? What do we prefer to forget? Those of very advanced years frequently forget what happened earlier that day but remember childhood with great clarity.

Occasionally, memories of past lives flash into the present. There's that sense of déjà vu with which many of us are familiar. There are stories of people who have experienced time slippages—could there be a connection here?

There are many with unexplained phobias in this present life. Why are so many frightened of snakes, water, spiders or mice? This type of fear can be explained by recognising that all four examples would have posed genuine threats to safety in numerous circumstances in the past, when life was far less comfortable. Some have unexplained anxiety, panic attacks, or fear of flying or heights. Many have flashbacks, memories so fleeting that there is no context for them—nothing but a feeling of (usually) terror, which is very unsettling. Often, they are quite unable to relax.

Visits to specialists can regress these patients into past lives, identifying scenes relevant to where the problem arose. Merely identifying the cause, and establishing the story, enables the person to work through and conquer the issue in his or her present life.

As spirits, we can choose to come to Earth (or elsewhere—that's a whole different theory!) on multiple occasions. In Hinduism, the soul is thought to work its way up, until perfection or the godlike state of Moksha is obtained. In Buddhism, this state is called Nirvana.

With Christianity, we are very short on information or guidance in regard to this rather fundamental life concept. It is very clear that as the early Christian church was organising itself, the gradually developing hierarchy realised that their rather enjoyable presence would be redundant if the general population saw no need for their intervention in order to pass on from the present life to something preferable. The Gnostics, who it has been suggested, practised a sort of rival Christianity were firm believers in reincarnation; but leaders of the early Church, specifically Irenaeus of Lyon, worked incredibly hard, and successfully, to suppress the Gnostics absolutely, long before the Council of Nicea. (See Chapter 4 for more detail).

In current times, our education levels allow us to embrace possibilities which once would have been considered heresy, and the idea of reincarnation is becoming widely acknowledged and mainstream. If, prior to reading these pages, you have been resistant to learning more, I gently invite you to suspend disbelief, at least while reading this short book. By the end of it, you might feel inspired to do your own research on this and other topics.

Even the word heresy has come to have a meaning different from the original. Going back to the time of Plato, Aristotle and so forth, heretics simply followed a particular branch of philosophy. The label became associated with dire punishment and threats of eternal damnation only when the Catholic Church was exerting its iron rule on followers and those who dared to murmur against its authority.

Yoga and Meditation

Both of these practices have a profound effect on those who discover them, but although introduced about 100 years ago to the West, there is still a huge percentage of people who have never tried either. Is it suspicion? Distrust? Laziness? Aversion to being exposed to a different faith in some way?

I recall, aged about 16, I had become rather intrigued with transcendental meditation (TM), and both my brother and I managed to persuade our mother to bring us along for a consultation. The three of us had a private discussion with a pleasant Indian man, aged about 40, in a small office on the outskirts of town. He invited us to return with a small fee, a white handkerchief, a flower and a couple of other symbolic items. Regrettably, we did not take things any further, because Mum recognised that this would involve another religion (shock! horror!) As Catholics, we were not even allowed to attend services of other Christian churches such as Methodist, Baptist, Anglican or whatever.

Recalling that the Beatles were proponents of TM and that they spent a year or so in India, where they learned meditation and yoga, I confirmed this online and discovered that it was George Harrison who had been the driving force. He wrote "My Sweet Lord" at this time, and set up the Radha Krishna Temple in Bloomsbury, London. In 1969, they released the *Hare Krishna* mantra in the UK, which had 4 airings on the BBC program Top of the Pops. It was the 1960s, the time of hippies and free love— was this perhaps when the "age of backpacking" began? There has certainly been a wave of travel-on-a-shoestring by young people to India, Tibet, Thailand and similar, often for purposes of learning Eastern practices and not just for tourism. It seems that many, if not most, settle down after their adventures, into suburbia and middle age.

I live in a sleepy village in Cambridgeshire. I used to work in an office in a nearby town, and I wasn't aware of any yoga classes nearby. Even now, live classes are fairly few and far between, and not convenient to access when working full time. Since lockdown, yoga classes have become readily available over the internet! In fact, we have all become so accustomed to doing so much at home, or from home, that I feel many of the new habits we have learned will persist even when we are free to move around again.

As time passes, the benefits of meditation are being recognised more and more. It's a procedure to calm the mind and, in so doing, the body is calmed as well. It's great for mental and emotional health, and reducing stress. Excellent for self-awareness, it helps lengthen the attention span, which can be an issue for busy people coping with information overload and overwhelm.

Studies have shown that meditation can help with age-related memory loss and help fight addictions through development of mental discipline. Meditation helps with pain control, blood pressure levels and can also reduce insomnia and improve sleep quality.

Yoga delivers all of the above but more so. It is a way of life, delivering the enlightenment of mind, body and soul. "Yoga" means union with God and has been practiced for over 5000 years with the ultimate goal of *moksha* or liberation.

There are numerous traditions, specialising in different types of yoga, of which there are 108! **Yogananda** practised Kriya yoga, which is highly specialised, taught one-to-one and for which teachers are not easily found. Breathing techniques are used to deliver the union of body and soul, renunciation, perception of self, access to the superconscious and *samadhi* (the state of unity with universal consciousness).

The Concept of Maya

I suspect that no discussion about the Eastern religions would be anywhere near complete without at least a reference to Maya, the word used to describe the limited, purely physical and mental reality in which our everyday consciousness has become entangled. The Hindu scriptures, the Upanishads, describe it at length. It is an illusion, a veiling of the true self—many spiritual trainers today speak of "piercing the veil," and this is where the expression originates.

The ego and karma are perceived as tools of Maya, who is referred to in the feminine, sometimes as Mother Maya. In order to achieve *moksha*, liberation of the soul from the cycle of death and rebirth, the illusion has to be overcome, and transcendental knowledge will effect this. Not having been raised in any of these traditions, I do not feel equipped to expound further; suffice it to say that explanations abound on the internet, most of which are very complex and hard to distil.

In recent years, there has been a considerable increase in the number of theories proposed in the West that also declare we are living in an illusion. Different terminologies are used, including simulation and virtual reality; in this age of the computer, it is much easier to grasp such ideas than it used to be. Apparently, it is impossible to prove that we are NOT living in a simulation. There was a popular theory a few years ago, called the Mandela Effect, which claimed to prove that something had gone wrong with the program, because large numbers of people had differing memories of past events, brands, logos and so on, which appeared to have changed with the passage of time. Paranormal events are explained as simply "glitches in the simulation." *The Matrix* trilogy, beginning in 1999, has convinced millions that simulation might be more than just a possibility. In fact, I recently heard **Dr Bruce Lipton** refer to it as a documentary.

Steve Jobs operated in a "reality distortion field," according to a new employee who was told that he was expected to comply with certain unrealistic expectations held by the CEO. He coined the description using *Star Trek* vocabulary, and it has since been quoted frequently to describe **Jobs'** personal refusal to accept limitations that stood in the way of his ideas. **Jobs** was able to convince himself that any difficulty was surmountable, and so strong was his vibration, enthusiasm and belief, that he was able to convince others that they, too, could achieve the impossible. It was an *internal* reality so powerful that it also became an *external* reality. This can be referred to as "mind hacking," and **Jobs** was a master hacker. Such was his personality that people around him were inspired to accept that anything he suggested was possible—at least in his presence. Apparently the effect wore off when he moved away...

Personal development trainers often quote **Henry Ford,** who said, *"If you think you can, or you think you can't, you're probably right."* You will be familiar with the term "self-fulfilling prophecy"—meaning that what we expect is what is most likely to happen. We can all deploy a personal distortion field and watch our reality change.

Earlier, I mentioned my intention to give some consideration to the topic of major world religions. In 2010, an estimated 82% of the world population followed some kind of religion. You might imagine that this figure would be declining, but rather surprisingly, the figure had increased to 84% by 2015, remaining the same in 2018. The next chapter summarises distribution of the major religions and compares adherence to a religion with the broader concept of spirituality.

Chapter 2

Religion and Spirituality

"In order to make the elevation towards religion easier for people, religion must be able to alter its forms in relation to the consciousness of modern man."
Aleksandr Solzhenitsyn

A Definition of Religion

I want to state very clearly that as I write, I am most definitely not setting out to offend anybody! My own perspective is Christian, as a result of my upbringing, but I truly believe that every religion has much to offer and that as we become more world-centric in our views and communications, humanity is recognising that most faiths are directed towards approximately the same goal: leading a good life on Earth with the intention of obtaining eventual eternal bliss of some sort, usually involving God. Unfortunately, some branches of religious fundamentalism and the sectarian violence such as that seen between Catholics and Protestants in Northern Ireland give religion a bad name. Throughout history, religious differences have caused numerous wars and the situation is ongoing, even today.

So what is the meaning of the word "religion?" Interestingly, there is a word in biochemistry—ligand—which means "to bind with a purpose." It does not seem to have a Latin root, although it sounds like it should have. Humans, being social animals, react very positively to having common interests and shared purposes, so when commentators refer to football, shopping or Facebook as being religions, this isn't a purely cynical use of the word.

Originally, in very primitive cultures, populations followed the sun god, the moon goddess, the river goddess and so on, and the purpose was for the common good. People knew that crops depended on weather and that they would suffer, or survive and thrive as a community according to whether or not the various gods looked upon them favourably. Over time, activities graduated from appeasement to worship, and as societies developed, more complex structures and hierarchies came into being to manage the environment, and the population.

Still standing today, we have Neolithic stone structures like Stonehenge and Avebury, Egyptian temples such as Edfu and Karnak, the pyramids, the incredible Inca ruins of Machu Picchu, the megaliths or giant statues on Easter Island in Polynesia and the NASCAR lines in Peru, to name some of the most famous. Apart from in Egypt, there was no form of writing, and so with the disappearance of the populations, so too were entire histories of the civilisations and peoples who built them lost to posterity.

Archaeologists conclude that these remaining structures indicate practices of worship by the different groups; in other words, the earliest religions. Whilst we know little detail, historians have pieced together theories about priestesses, vestal virgins and sacrifices. One of the oldest written historic records is the Bible, and of course we have the hieroglyphs of Egypt, which were a mystery until the discovery of the famous Rosetta Stone. This contains details of a priestly decree issued in Memphis, Egypt, in 196 BC. It was the key to deciphering hieroglyphs, as the decree had also been recorded on the stone in Demotic and Ancient Greek, which were well known to scholars.

Although present day knowledge of ancient religions is sketchy, they clearly had structures in common with the large religions of later times: that is, hierarchy and control. It would seem that in times past, when education was not widely available, the general population had little choice other than to submit to control by those higher up the food chain. Summarising what will have happened at different rates in different cultures, people became interested in what was in store for them after they died. Those already better placed will have recognised an opportunity to enhance their own positions by convincing acknowledged leaders that they alone had methods of appeasing the gods, foretelling events and eventually helping to control populations. The idea that one's behaviour whilst alive dictated one's comfort after death, provided enormous leverage.

Similarities Throughout the Ages

The idea that God or the gods could see you, even when no one else could, was brilliant in terms of governing behaviour. Take this even further—that God can read your mind and that "thou shalt not covet"—let alone do anything about it; combine this with threats of eternal damnation and the flames of hell, and no wonder the population, broadly speaking, toed the line.

I refer of course to the Ten Commandments, given by the God of the Old Testament to Moses, which define how a person can live a life pleasing to God. Sixty per cent of them set out rules for a stable society. The remainder are instructions about how the God of Abraham insisted on being worshipped.

The majority of religions followed today either worship God or at least acknowledge him. Christianity worships Jesus Christ as the Only Son of God, being part of the Holy Trinity along with the Holy Spirit. Many others, including those originating in India, Persia and Arabia, acknowledge Christ as a major prophet or saint, but not as the Son of God.

It's interesting to look at how the traditions of the early Christians of the Levant (broadly what we call the Middle East today) have intermingled with existing practices of the many so-called mystery religions of the area. The Roman army, while occupying Britannia in the first four centuries, built temples to Mithras, who was originally Persian. Remains can be seen at sites and museums along the ruins of Hadrian's Wall in Northumbria. Little is known about Mithras, although some say his life story was similar to Christ's. This is unproven, because it was a mystery religion, and little was ever written down.

Pagan religions were in existence throughout the Empire, and they were absorbed by the Roman machine. To make the process as seamless as possible, many Pagan practices were subsumed into Christianity. For example, 25th December was appropriated as Christ's birthday, as there were already celebrations established in respect of the winter solstice, or shortest day. The mistletoe, under which it is traditional to steal a kiss, was an integral part of Celtic folklore and sacred to the

Druids. Because of this, it was once not allowed in Christian churches. The word "pagan" became a derogatory term, referring to one who was outside of any religion, and therefore uncivilised.

Modern Religions

Catholics are still expected to attend Mass every Sunday and on certain holy days of obligation. I am uncertain as to whether or not eating meat on Fridays is currently forbidden—that rule seems to pop in and out of favour—but for centuries, because Catholicism was so widespread, all institutions would habitually offer a fish meal on the menu on Fridays.

When Henry VIII failed to obtain permission from the Pope to divorce Catherine of Aragon in order to marry Anne Boleyn, he broke away from Rome and proclaimed himself head of the English Church. The Sovereign is today still head of the Church of England (C of E). Anglicanism is the "High Church" variant of C of E, and their services are very close to those of the Catholics. C of E are less splendid, and their churches and ceremonies tend to be simpler. Little is demanded of adherents, but services such as christenings, marriages and funerals (or hatches, matches and despatches) are available.

Twenty years ago, when the UK census figures for 2001 were compiled, I recall hearing comments about how the totals of people declaring their allegiance to any specific religion were declining with each decade—no surprises there. But in the section denoting "Other – please specify," there had been a remarkable number declaring themselves as Jedi Knights—no fewer than 390 thousand! This apparently was the result of a prank: a widely distributed email campaign had inspired numerous young people to declare themselves as such, following on from the popularity of the recently revived *Star Wars* franchise.

Joking apart, considering that an estimated 84% of the world's population self-identify as believers, how many major world religions can you name? I located a pie chart depicting the distribution in 2015, which I found very enlightening. Starting with Christianity—this accounts for nearly half of the pie—those missionaries were very effective! (Actually, there's a darker backstory to the spread of Christianity, which went hand in hand with conquest of distant lands and genocides of a sort, but I will not be discussing that here.) Roman Catholicism accounted for 25%, and while enthusiasm has been declining for many years, especially in the light of the child abuse scandals (which are not confined to the Catholics incidentally), there is a saying, "Once a Catholic, always a Catholic." This is because unless active conversion to another faith occurs, one is considered to remain a so-called lapsed Catholic.

Christians of other, mainly Protestant varieties together account for another 24%. In descending order of magnitude, the groups comprise Orthodox Eastern, Protestants (including C of E), African Indigenous sects, Anglicans, Pentecostalists and Baptists. Together comprising less than 1% on the pie are Jehovah's Witnesses, Quakers and numerous American sects. Christianity developed from Judaism, but although the Jewish religion is widely spread across the world, in addition to within Israel itself, this comprises only 0.2% of the world population. Frequently, commentators refer to "Judeo-Christianity," and the two of these, together with Islam, are referred to as the "Abrahamic religions" because all follow the God of the Old Testament, in which Abraham is an important character.

The fastest growing religion today is Islam (adherents are called Muslims). Their 25% of the pie (2015) comprised mainly Sunni with a very much smaller component of Shiite Muslims.

Hinduism, of which there are 2 branches, accounts for 19%, and Buddhism, which grew out of Hinduism and also has 2 main branches, accounts for 7%. We are already up to 100%, and I haven't even mentioned Jainism, Shintoism, Confucianism, Taoism, Zoroastrianism, Native American sects, Wicca, Pagan religions and probably several more. Sikhism just crept onto the pie chart at "less than 1%," but thanks to rounding, would have brought our total up to 101%.

So whilst the percentages given will have changed, as they were compiled five years ago from several sources, they nevertheless give an idea of world belief systems and the huge percentage who follow some sort of religion rather than nothing at all.

Control Systems

Common to all religions are restrictions on individual freedom, and rules and regulations which are in many cases, quite onerous. The vast majority of those who profess to follow a religion were born into families that had embraced that particular faith for generations, and so have unquestioningly lived with the teachings from earliest years. Attendance at schools that teach the same dogma, and weekly attendance at a church, temple, mosque or applicable meeting place, ensures that the programming is efficiently assimilated.

In parts of the West, the system is collapsing, as societies become more secular, often to the consternation of dyed-in-the-wool older generations, many of whom were brought up themselves in different countries. In the West, overt control has been falling out of favour for at least half a century in all areas: absence of the death penalty, no corporal punishment in schools and even laws that restrict how parents may discipline their own offspring at home. It follows that young people will tend not to choose to follow pathways that restrict their freedoms.

In many religions, comfort has never been part of the mix. Modern societies value "choice" and "speaking my truth" (as opposed to "the truth"?). In the first half of the last century, in the UK, schoolchildren were routinely beaten for not being able to recite chunks of the Catechism. This was a Catholic inter-pretation of the teachings of the Bible and consisted of hundreds of questions and answers which had to be learnt by heart. Fortunately, this practice had long fallen away by the time I went to school! Catholics, incidentally, were not encouraged to read the Bible—nor discouraged—it was simply the book from which priests and ministers would read at church services, a repository of the stories known as parables, and records of Christ's life and ministry as recorded in the four gospels. The rest of the New Testament remained more or less a mystery, but we were aware of the Psalms, the Epistles and the most famous books of the Old Testament, namely Genesis and Moses.

Analysts frequently credit the fact that education levels in modern civilisations have risen so high that people no longer "need" religion for guidance. A slant on this is that people have learned to think, and therefore reject some of the more absurd teachings of whatever religion they were born into. Others amongst us believe that laziness is key—that younger generations couldn't be bothered, or can't find the time to fit religious practices into their lives. Still others pay lip service to religion, in order to avoid arguments with their parents. Many take a few years off, then return to whatever tradition when children come along, as there is little doubt that growing up with a framework for life is a good idea.

The rise of materialism and the decline of religion have coincided. For plenty of people, money has become their god and shopping their religion. Suppose you have no belief in any kind of life after death—why not enjoy yourself to the fullest during your time on Earth? It's a pretty short time, after all, and there's no argument against the statement, "You can't take it with you."

Money, in the form of debt, is what controls most of us in our current lives. Unfortunately, we live in a world where success is defined by income. Admit that you are short of money, and you are declaring that you are a loser—and there is the widespread pressure to "keep up with the Joneses." Hence, the tendency to spend more than we can afford, and this is why so many of us get into consumer debt, from which it can be so difficult to escape. In addition, in many societies, there is the expectation that we should take on a mortgage as soon as possible, which locks in a heavy obligation to repay a sizeable loan, for years into the future.

The majority just don't know how money works and how heavily everything is stacked in the favour of the banks. At school, we might learn a formula for calculating compound interest, but it isn't clarified that this compounding effect explains why it is so very difficult to get out of consumer debt. Banks charge interest, and then interest on interest, at high rates, and they win every time. Compounding is available to savers, but the rates need to be above 6% for the magic to kick in—few investments pay that nowadays.

The System is designed to keep us all on the hamster treadmill— we are too busy or too frightened to jump off. Too many middle-income people are quietly firefighting, living month to month, hoping nothing happens to rock the boat (or capsize it completely). Very many families, aspirational or not, can no longer manage long term on one income. Both partners have to work. The lie is that this gives women freedom and independence—it isn't necessarily the case! Fine if the kids are older and the second partner is a career person working for choice, but what about when expensive childcare has to be funded, that accounts for a large part of the second income?

What about the countless partners taking home the minimum wage, hardly seeing their kids, being tired all the time, with no energy to keep house, cook properly or spend quality time with the family? Plenty of grandparents feel obligated to help out with childcare—and even when they are compensated under semi-formal arrangements, it still represents a brake on the freedoms that they might have been anticipating. **Henry David Thoreau**, an American philosopher writing in the mid-19th century, said: "The majority of people are living lives of quiet desperation," and regrettably this is more true than ever today.

Spirituality

Most of us will have been told when growing up that we were a body and that we possessed a soul. In other words, our existence was our body—the physical flesh and blood—which would eventually die. At this time, our souls would leave our bodies and, provided we had lived good lives and followed the rules, then our souls would be allowed entry into heaven.

In past ages, the teaching was that those who died in a state of sinfulness would have to reside in purgatory while they repented and atoned, eventually earning the privilege of admittance to heaven. If there were no repentance, then there was no hope for the soul—it would suffer eternal damnation and burn forever in hell. Such beliefs kept populations in line for centuries, but significant relaxation was already occurring in the last century. Hell was now the undesirable state of everlasting separation from God. Heaven would not be unreasonably withheld from anyone.

So many questions remained unanswered by this philosophy. Our souls would be happy with God forever. And ever. And ever. Wouldn't we get bored? No—boredom wouldn't exist in heaven. God always was and always will be. Okay, so the idea of "never-ending," like the number pi (3.141592…), is understandable, but never starting? Our human minds struggle with the concept.

So let's change the perspective. Rather than being a body with a soul, your essence is the soul itself, and it is occupying the body for a length of time. Now, if we are all spiritual beings having a brief experience on Earth… it's the body (and not the soul) that has a beginning and end. We are told that we are made in God's image (nobody knows what God looks like). We do not know what our souls look like either! If we consider our souls as being individuations of God (rather than individuals), then we realise just how much we have in common with every other being on the planet—indeed with every being previously, or yet to be on the planet.

So the physical Universe is separate from the spiritual Universe. Some prefer to talk about "the Universe" rather than God. God is everywhere, and everything, so why not? Others use terms such as the Divine, All That There Is, the Creator, or Source. I rather like the term **George Lucas** used in *Star Wars:* "May the Force be with you!" For the rest of the following narrative, because most of the world is familiar with the term, I will be referring to God. In doing so, I do *not* refer to the angry, white-haired old man as depicted in sundry Old Testament illustrations!

Because we inhabit a planet whirling in space, which experiences not only night and day but different seasons in the course of a year, it's natural that we would need to measure time. Einstein told us about relativity and the space-time continuum. So mankind shakily grasped the concept that time wasn't real. You may have heard it described as a human construct. If you appreciate that it exists only in the physical Universe and not in the spiritual Universe, this greatly assists in explaining the concept of infinity—having no beginning or end—as represented by the number eight sideways on.

Faith healing, alternative medicine and extra sensory perception are easier to understand when we recognise how much power is available to us when we simply look within ourselves.

Spirituality means getting in touch with our Spirit selves— appreciating who we really are—and recognising the true meaning of life. As a species, there is little doubt that we are awakening. There is a whole new paradigm gradually becoming known to greater numbers of people. What's more, scientists are supporting this knowledge and are recognising that what has been taught for centuries in Eastern cultures is actually in alignment with modern quantum physics.

Consciousness and the Divine Matrix

The idea of the conscience is pretty universal—it's that little voice in our heads that tells us when we are breaking the rules, being judgemental or having bad thoughts. In other words, it is our sense of morality, of right and wrong.

When I first heard the term "higher self"—and I believe that this was not that many years ago, when I attended a course on Theta Healing—I recall that I linked the idea with conscience. I now recognise that my higher self is my spirit self. In psychology, they use the terms id, ego and superego, with conscience being part of the superego. In biology, the distinctions are subconscious, conscious and superconscious. In theology, we speak of body, mind and spirit. Clearly, spirit is the soul. The conscious mind is the intellect, or what we use to be aware of anything. Conscious is the adjective from which the noun consciousness comes. But consciousness is not the mind—it is the awareness of being. It is the underlying essence of everything.

To be conscious is to be awake, or to be aware. As consciousness develops, we become aware of, or awakened to, a more complete picture of the situation as it really is. This is the great awakening that is happening now, as gradually we perceive the truth of our presence here on Earth. For completeness, I would point out that being "awakened" is the absolute opposite of being "woke," which is nothing but a trendy, misguided and closed-minded position adopted by sections of society with issues they prefer to blame on the generalised other.

So, the truth of our situation is that we are spiritual beings occupying (a succession of) human bodies, and we are part of an enormous whole. Try and describe the size of the galaxies visible in the night sky, and you get a sense of the vastness. Spiritual masters have known this for centuries, but the wisdom is only now, slowly trickling down to the general population. Earlier generations probably could not have appreciated the knowledge. Yet we know that there were civilisations in the distant past which disappeared without a trace, but which had technologies that we have still not attained. Theories estimate that the human race has destroyed itself (or been wiped out) more or less, around six times. Some suggest that we are approaching the sixth in the present time.

In **Lynne McTaggert's** book *The Field,* she tells the fascinating and detailed story of how scientists had essentially closed their minds to possibilities outside of where perceived wisdom—or rather, accepted theories—had arrived by the 1970s. Early pioneers were mocked—disgraced even—as they dared to publish any new, divergent theories within the scientific community.

The enormous whole is referred to variously as the Zero Point Field, the Unified Field, the Quantum Field, or just the Field, the

Matrix or the Divine Matrix, and there are probably several other terms for it. It is the science of the miraculous, the scientific validation of what used to be explained using the word "miracle." This knowledge is the next revolution, and it is in progress right now. It provides an explanation for how prayer works, and how group meditation has the same causative effect. We are all connected, all part of the matrix. The ocean is made up of individual drops of water, but they coalesce together and there is no separation. So it is with our souls, although we *appear* to have separate identities whilst inhabiting these physical bodies.

As science and spirituality are gradually forming a truce, and recognising that many of their beliefs and observations are in harmony with one another, the world is experiencing the fastest growth in knowledge, information and capability in recorded history. It's an exciting time to be alive and to be participating in the growth and availability, but perception and perspective will both be beneficial as we navigate this new landscape. In the next chapter, I will be discussing secrecy, suppression and subterfuge, so I invite you to continue the journey with me.

Chapter 3

What Is Truth?

"A lie which is half a truth is ever the blackest of lies."
Alfred Lord Tennyson

History – As Written by the Victors

When you think of Richard III, what springs to mind? Maybe the fact that this is the name of one of **Shakespeare's** better known plays? Or perhaps you have a mental picture of a grossly deformed hunchback with an evil, sneering grin? The two things are connected: Shakespeare was writing during the time of Queen Elizabeth I, who was a Tudor monarch. The Tudor line had begun with her grandfather, Henry VII, when the Wars of the Roses finally ended.

You may also think of King Richard III as the murderer of the two young princes who had been held prisoner in the Tower of London. This was much more probably a story circulated by Henry VII and his supporters as they attempted to consolidate his position as the new king. Research by respected historians has shown that in fact Richard III was not quite the warped cripple described by Shakespeare. He was a decent person and a skilled warrior, who unfortunately suffered from scoliosis, or curvature of the spine. This is a painful condition, but it's unlikely that Richard was a total cripple, for this would have made him unable to take an active part in any fighting.

Incidentally, Richard was killed in the last battle of the Wars of the Roses and buried without ceremony in the grounds of a local abbey. His skeleton was located in 2012, in what was by then a car park in the city of Leicester, amidst great excitement and publicity. The remains were positively identified using DNA testing, and then at long last he was laid to rest, as befitted a king, in Leicester Cathedral. There had been some debate about his deserving, as a king, to be buried at Westminster Abbey, but Leicester won the argument and claimed him as their own.

Back in in 1485, when the Wars of the Roses came to an end, even the printing press had not been invented. No mass media at all was in operation. Any books were painstakingly hand copied by monks, and most were housed in cathedral libraries or monasteries. Only the rich and well connected received any sort of education. Therefore "news" consisted of rumours skilfully circulated by those with an agenda. Any kind of hard evidence was difficult to produce. Consider the ill-fated Queen Anne Boleyn (wife of Henry VIII, and Elizabeth's mother), who received a parody of a trial and was executed for treason in 1536. And so were the unfortunate (and almost certainly innocent) men accused of being her lovers. The sort of proof that was acceptable in a court of law in those days, to our modern standards, looks ridiculously flimsy. It usually consisted of "confessions," frequently extracted under torture, and copied down by scribes paid by the people extracting the evidence.

When I was at school, I enjoyed history, and I believed what we were taught. In the main, it really didn't occur to me to question any of it. For example, ask anybody these days how the bubonic plague proliferated in England in 1665, and (assuming they had learnt about it at all) they will tell you confidently that it wasn't spread by rats, but by the fleas on the rats! However, research recently has shown that it's much more likely to have been spread by human fleas or even body lice. Ugh! We are told that the great fire of London, the following year, started by accident in a cookhouse on Pudding Lane. It is much more likely that the fire was methodically started on purpose by the authorities, with a view to cleansing the city and preventing a recurrence of the pestilence.

Hollywood and film studios of all nationalities have played their parts in the massaging of history. You will be familiar with the countless films that have been produced in Hollywood, both during and after World War II, depicting stories of how the Americans came across to Britain to lend a hand and proceeded to turn the course of the war for the Allies. In most of the film scripts, they triumph more or less unaided. However, the British film industry gives rather more credit to the British! Naturally, each country will have its own take on how events transpired, and where to apportion blame or credit. Some months ago, I was directed to a film on YouTube called *Hellstorm*, which describes what happened after the end of World War II, from the German point of view. That documentary film has excellent credentials, and the content is graphic and gruesome, showing the Russians, the Americans and specifically Eisenhower in a shockingly bad light. This film is the clearest of demonstrations of history being written by the victors.

Democracy, and "one man, one vote," is unquestionably a busted flush. So-called oppressed populations don't realise that this generally means "one man, one vote, once only." We very frequently hear about elections held, usually in third world countries, where the losing party complains that the result has been "stolen" by the proclaimed victor. At best, the cries of unfairness, or underhand practices, go ignored. At worst, the leader of the losing party is quietly disposed of after the passage of a few months or years. Potentially, members of his or her family may be threatened, even killed—to the extent that the challenger recognises defeat or just loses the will to continue. Even several decades ago, before the technologies sometimes blamed today, elections in Africa produced some very questionable results. But what can be done? If the result solves a political problem, or divests one country of a responsibility it no longer wants, then all is considered well in the name of expediency.

Theories, Conspiracies and Fake News

In 1984, I was living in the UK, essentially on my own, having left Hong Kong where my parents lived as expats at the time. I was then a bright-eyed, unsophisticated accountancy trainee, with little time for anything other than work or study, who was still very much under the influence of my upbringing. This had been in Africa where I had attended a Catholic School.

One of the other residents in the shared house where I lived had recommended the book *Holy Blood Holy Grail*—a non-fiction work which had been on the bestseller list 2 years previously— but I had never heard of it. Just then I was auditing in London, which meant an hour-long train commute each way. I recall vividly looking forward to those journeys, reading this incredible theory that Jesus and Mary Magdalene had been husband and wife, and that she had escaped to the south of France after the crucifixion, whilst expecting a child! She thus carried within her the sacred bloodline, from which the Merovingian dynasty was descended. A raft of secret societies, including the Priory of Sion, Opus Dei and the Knights Templar, had all been set up for the purpose of keeping this bloodline secret.

I found that book to be more of a page turner than any thriller or who-dunnit, and I even wondered if I was some sort of heretic for daring to read and actually consider the possibility of what was a very plausibly presented hypothesis. The writers did not claim to offer actual proof, but as they carefully disclosed their research and unwrapped their evidence, it certainly proved to be very convincing.

Some twenty years later, **Dan Brown** had the brainwave of presenting exactly the same information in the format of a thriller-mystery novel, and *The Da Vinci Code* became the fastest selling fiction publication of all time. It way outsold the original and introduced an enormous contemporary audience to information which has caused the religious establishment considerable concern, this time around.

Holy Blood Holy Grail had been my very first exposure to a "conspiracy theory," and it was extremely compelling. Within a month, I was back in Hong Kong on my annual home visit, so naturally I presented my mother with a copy of the book. (Back then, there was no Amazon, no Skype or Zoom, and our occasional long distance phone calls were expensive, with obvious time constraints.) After my visit ended, Mum read the book, was utterly horrified by it and wrote to a Bishop in the UK—probably for advice regarding how to counteract the arguments—and wanting to know what action the Church was taking within Christian communities. His response was dismissive, unconvincing and extremely disappointing. I think the Church merely waited for any furore to just die down, as it tends to do after any nine-day wonder.

In 2006, the authors of *Holy Blood Holy Grail,* **Michael Baigent, Leigh Richard and Henry Lincoln,** sued **Dan Brown** for plagiarism, and lost. Nevertheless, the court case caused renewed interest in their research, and substantial additional sales of both books. Another conspiracy, possibly?

When President John F Kennedy was assassinated in 1963, the official story of his death, as presented to a shocked American public, satisfied them only for a very short while. His killer was quickly named as Lee Harvey Oswald, who was conveniently shot by Jack Ruby, before Oswald could stand trial. Oswald had worked for the CIA, which might have had secrets to hide! Hypotheses were circulating wildly, and the CIA dismissed these as "conspiracy theories." This was the birth of one of the all-time greatest put-downs. It was relatively easy to contain undesirable information in an age where mass media could be controlled. Since the rise of the internet, such containment has become totally impossible.

With this challenge has arisen a parallel problem: fake news. How are we supposed to distinguish the truthful from the scurrilous? In **George Orwell's** book *Nineteen Eighty Four,* the protagonist, Winston, works for the Ministry of Truth (which in new-speak meant un-truth), and his job was to work through government archives, removing content no longer favourable to Big Brother and replacing it with false information. **Orwell** was remarkably prescient, and even foresaw television, but I wonder what he would make of the internet? It would be Big Brother's dream, and has already changed our concept of censorship (see Chapter 8).

Who Do You Trust?

Bad news sells papers. So does sensationalism. Anyone whose livelihood depends on sales of any type of media knows this only too well. In April 1917, the *Times* and the *Daily Mail* published accounts from anonymous sources who claimed to have visited the Kadaververwertungsanstalt, or corpse-utilisation factory, in Germany. The original story had been translated, but whilst the German text had referred in fact to bodies of dead animals, the benefit of a mistranslation, that suggested a ghastly end in store for dead soldiers, would be an ideal addition to wartime anti-German propaganda.

Germany protested loudly, of course, but was not believed. The Chinese were so outraged at the idea, that it caused them to abandon their neutral position, and China declared war against Germany in August of that year. Much later, it was admitted that there had been a department within the British Ministry of Information which was devoted to producing exactly this kind of misinformation, and one of their intentions had been to bring China into the war.

But lies have consequences. During the 1930s, the corpse factory lie was used by the Nazis as proof of British lies during the 1914–18 war. And early reports of the holocaust under Hitler in World War II were not believed, on the same basis.

Suppose we were told today, by a reliable source, that a certain country had stores of weapons of mass destruction. Following on from the deceptions that led to the second Gulf War, the "dodgy dossier" and so forth, it's doubtful that we would be easily convinced. Yet although in some cases we have become supremely sceptical, in others we can be remarkably gullible. There is the famous story of an April Fools' Day prank, carried out by **Richard Dimbleby** and the team at the end of his respected current affairs program. It seems incredible in this cosmopolitan age, but in 1957, it worked brilliantly. A 2 ½ minute film was prepared, detailing how spaghetti was harvested from trees in Italy. They hung soft, homemade spaghetti from the branches of numerous laurel trees, and filmed it being cut down, laid out in the sun to dry, and packaged up for sale in shops. One reason that so many were taken in is that Mr Dimbleby was a "revered and trusted public figure."

Joking apart, it is a well-known fact that on matters of health, we are more likely to believe someone wearing a white coat with a stethoscope around his neck, than someone wearing jeans and a T-shirt. **Robert Cialdini** has written two famous books, *Influence* and *Pre-suasion*, which are used like bibles by the advertising profession. Millions of us have studied neuro-linguistic programming, a subtle method of convincing others to do as we want by using certain speech patterns and carefully chosen words. The problem is, it has become harder and harder to trust anybody. The long-running TV series *The X Files* warned us every week to "trust no one." But after all, it was a program about conspiracy theories.

The internet is rife with alternative news coverage, conspiracy theories and fake news. Which is which? How are they identified? The Establishment wants us to believe that 5G is perfectly safe. During the early stages of the first UK lockdown, it was considered to be an excellent time to erect countless 5G masts, because nobody was looking. When the ruse became known, suddenly "conspiracy theorists" launched arson attacks on numerous masts.

Sound arguments and concerns against 5G were bundled together with anxieties about the spread of the virus pandemic—indeed, there could be a connection—but reasoned discussions outlining the dangers of 5G have been banned outright. The subject is not allowed to be debated on mainstream media, so naturally, people were going to turn to YouTube and social media for information. The algorithms went mad! People realised that even uttering the words would probably lead to their articles being taken down. Violence is never the answer; the arsonists did nobody any favours. But the question is, when did critical thinking become conspiracy theory?

As a footnote to the 5G story, while all this was going on in April 2020, there were daily broadcasts advising the population of the national COVID-19 situation, and one particular day, a presenter summarised the story of the attacks and asked one of the other government representatives, who might have been a doctor but probably wasn't, "What do you think about these so-called dangers of 5G?" The answer, not surprisingly, was along the lines of, "Well, it's all absolute rubbish." And that was it; answer considered satisfactory. No evidence, no background, no facts. And there was never any more discussion on the subject.

Education or Indoctrination?

Schoolchildren have minds like sponges, especially in the early years. They often believe that their teachers are genuinely expert in whatever topic is being discussed, and so tend not only to accept everything that they are told, but to remember discrete pieces of information as "truth" for their whole lives. As they grow older, pupils generally become more challenging and argumentative, but this is more often than not for reasons of boredom, or showing off to their peers. My first chosen career was as a high school teacher of science and mathematics, and during my post-grad teacher training, one of our set books was called *Teaching as a Subversive Activity.* It was in no way political! The point that the book made was that teachers needed to be aware of the power that their words and views could have.

In fact, discussion and questioning should be encouraged in school, but this is usually relegated to the Debating Society, perhaps because in most subjects there simply is not the time available to do much more than cover the syllabus. This is no accident. There really is a great deal of room for improvement in the education system, as with each passing year, it becomes less and less fit for purpose. Schools train behaviour, rather than intellect. Children are seldom taught to think and are instructed to memorise, rather than to learn. "Learning by rote" is an expression—it is not actual learning! Students are rewarded for passing exams—generally achieved by regurgitating masses of memorised information. Those with good memories do well; those without are seen as less intelligent.

The left side of the brain deals with logic, systems, memory and structure. By the time I completed my academic education, I was expert at passing exams, and as I have since realised, my left brain had been enthusiastically over-developed. This, sadly, was at the expense of the right side, which deals with creativity, dreaming, individuality and the qualities that make us more interesting, rounded members of society. Ideally, both sides of the brain should develop in tandem, but I do not believe that a standard education is designed to achieve this kind of result.

Moreover, the opinions and perceptions to which students are exposed whilst at school, very much tend to stay with them throughout their lives, and those who design curricula are well aware of this. For example, thinking about Guy Fawkes and the plot to assassinate King James I, "remember, remember, the 5th of November..."

This infamous drama was part of the culmination of more than a century of conflict between the Catholics and Protestants in England. Scottish King James I, the Protestant monarch who succeeded Elizabeth I, was exceedingly unpopular with Catholics, who were sneeringly known as Papists. From the earliest months of his reign, he had stepped up persecution against them, and there had been a horrifying increase in the numbers of executions. Fawkes was a Catholic, and he and his men plotted against the King and the Establishment, attempting to blow up the Houses of Parliament on 5 November, 1605. Fawkes and his gang were caught, horribly tortured and then hung, drawn and quartered, which was the punishment for treason at the time. The king's escape from assassination was celebrated by the lighting of bonfires, and a decree was issued that it should be so celebrated every year.

The next monarch (Charles I, who was executed by Parliament in 1649) had Catholic sympathies, and then after 14 years of Protectorate under Cromwell, his Catholic son, Charles II, reigned and was generally popular. But religious tensions were still rife, and Charles' very unpopular son, James II, was the final Catholic king of England. It is now even written into English law that no Catholic may reign—in fact, a Catholic may not even marry into the royal family!

How delightful that there should be such an exciting story about a Catholic villain, available for consumption by schoolchildren. Even in the current climate, where a majority of the population holds no particular religious convictions, and religion is not overtly taught in secular schools, this underlying bias is casually implanted in the heads of generations of pupils.

Particularly in the UK, and the USA, parents and children have been convinced that milk is good for them. It even used to be distributed free of charge in schools, and its virtues were enthusiastically described by (misguided) teachers. This was down to clever and well-financed advertising campaigns rather than scientific fact. I have more to say about the lies of the food industry, in Chapter 8.

It isn't only schools that are masters of the art of subtle influence. Soap operas have successfully been used by governments to persuade populations in certain directions.

There used to be public information advertisements, persuading drivers to wear seatbelts, for example. Obviously, news broadcasts also fulfil this teaching, or brainwashing, function very successfully, but not everyone watches the news...

Schools and colleges are sausage machines, designed to turn out workers rather than thinkers. The more academic students are expected to progress upwards to further or higher education, and achieve expensive qualifications. This usually involves taking on debt, unless parents are wealthy or have planned for the expenditure. For many years now, I have questioned the value of mine—but that has been the System for over a century. It needs to change. The fast changing pace of the last couple of decades demonstrates this very clearly, and the situation is escalating at an ever-increasing rate.

The Dead Sea Scrolls

Possibly one of the most significant and best-known archaeological events of the last century was the discovery of the Dead Sea Scrolls. Jars containing texts, which had been hidden in caves in the desert at Qumran, about an hour from Jerusalem, were found by Bedouins in 1947 and sold for the sum of $250 to a local Orthodox priest. Little more was heard of them until, in 1954, an advertisement appeared in the Wall Street Journal, which was seen by a travelling Israeli archaeologist. Immediately, he recognised their significance and purchased the scrolls for $250,000! They had been smuggled at some time into the United States, and he was delighted to be able to purchase them on behalf of his country. Once the location of the find had been established, archaeologists flocked back to the area and, by 1956, another eleven caves had been found.

In all, more than 800 scripts were located, written in a variety of languages, including Aramaic, Greek and Latin. The first scrolls, which had appeared in America, were almost identical to the existing Old Testament. But the newly found collection of texts was clearly a library: There were more Old Testament writings, accounts of everyday life (this was the period of the Second Temple) and there was also a group of writings referred to as the Sectarian Scrolls. These had been written by a group calling themselves the Sons of Light, between the 3rd century BC and the first century AD.

In the 1950s, carbon dating was very new, and there was reluctance to use it on these precious historical documents; but in time, carbon-14 testing was invented, and the documents have since been conclusively dated back to the first century AD and earlier. We know little about the Sons of Light, but it seems that being in touch with angels was a significant part of their religious practice. Numerous writers have proposed theories about the Sons of Light, possibly starting with Pliny, who refers to them as the Essenes back in the first century BC. It seems that they were a Hermetic sect (see the next chapter), that their dwellings were communal, their elders probably lived monastically and their desert existence was harsh and ascetic.

The Sectarian Scrolls collection includes the War Scroll, which relates how the people were awaiting a final conflict against the Sons of Darkness. Jewish history, as summarised in the Old Testament, contains obvious gaps, but other writers around the time, combined with numerous archaeological studies, provide a reasonably comprehensive historical background as to why the scrolls might have been hidden. The Second Jewish Revolt happened in 66–70 AD, culminating in the total destruction of Jerusalem and the Temple. The population was either slaughtered or sold into slavery, so if the scrolls had been hidden out in the desert for safety, it is likely that no one survived to reclaim them.

Characters within the War Scroll are codified—there is, for example, the Wicked Priest, the Teacher of Righteousness, and the Man of Lies. Attempts have been made to identify Jesus and John the Baptist with these characters. **John Lash's** *Not in His Image* (2006) contains a vast amount of detail about the scrolls, and theories about the character of Jesus. **Barbara Thiering** published *Jesus the Man* in 1991, which contains the theory that Jesus did not die on the cross, but married Mary Magdalen—a variation on the *Holy Blood Holy Grail* theory discussed earlier. In one of the caves, the jars had not survived, and so the texts that remained were on mere fragments of papyrus. Much of the translation (and detective work), prior to the 1990s, was carried out by Catholics and in secret, giving rise to many conspiracy theories and never-proven rumours.

There is no question that the Vatican has vast Secret Archives—and speculation as to exactly what lies within is rife. For example, two famous appearances of Mary, Mother of God, to Bernadette at Lourdes and to three children at Fatima, involve disclosures about the future of the planet. Much of that information is withheld, even after more than a century, indicating that the Vatican still considers that they dare not reveal these prophesies. The secrecy involved in suppressing the scroll translations, and limiting expert access to the physical scrolls, stoked controversy for decades, and there are many books available—plus countless lectures on YouTube—which document the frustration felt at the time, leading back to the problem of what is genuine and what is speculation. Early investigations were done by Christians, who rather naturally saw the scrolls within a particular context and were unwilling for outsiders to have the ability to come up with alternative theories and conclusions.

Even in the current climate of "freedom of information," it is very apparent that uncovering the truth remains a considerable challenge. Truth, illusion, delusion, perception, misconception... It seems that a great many prefer to accept conformity and a peaceful life, following instructions and never asking difficult questions. But if you have a more enquiring mind, I invite you to read on. In the next chapter, I will be discussing one of the most successfully suppressed belief systems of recent history.

Chapter 4

The Story of Sophia

"It's not what you look at that matters, it's what you see."
Henry David Thoreau

The Nag Hammadi Codices

In Nag Hammadi, Egypt, right at the end of 1945, a cache of sealed jars containing texts was found by a local peasant. Eventually most, but sadly not all, found their way to the Coptic Museum in Cairo. The texts were contained in thirteen leather bound codices (codex being the Roman word for book) rather than scrolls, as were found at the Dead Sea location. Once again, because of the state of decay and fragmentation, it was many years before translations became widely available. The Nag Hammadi find is less well known, however, probably because rather less secrecy and argument attaches to the publication of their contents.

Some refer to the texts, of which there are over 50, as the Gnostic Gospels, possibly because the name of the first English translation, published by **Elaine Pagels** in 1976, was *The Gnostic*

Gospels. Gnosticism is seen by many as a branch of early Christianity, whilst others call it a parallel religion of the time. Whichever is accurate, Gnosticism has been ferociously suppressed since the second century AD. It had more or less disappeared into oblivion by the 4th century, when Christianity became the official religion of the Roman Empire (Chapter 2). The texts were written in Greek and Coptic, and modern translations began to appear only in the 1970s. Apparently, many of the texts are themselves translations from other languages into Coptic, which was spoken in Egypt at the time. The Gnostic tradition is known to have been widespread in Egypt and the Levant.

The 1970 publications encouraged much interest in Gnosticism because it presents as a missing link—long lost pieces of a puzzle—new information about the early followers of Jesus Christ. Some of the writings had been known about but had been presumed lost. In 1896, fragments of the Gospel of Mary Magdalen had been found, in which she is described as "the beloved disciple," to whom had been revealed secret instructions about life, death, heaven and the journey of the soul after death. She is presented as a person of insight, a leader. It is believed that she did not write the gospel herself, but that the information had been transcribed by a Gnostic. The Gnostics embraced women as full members of the community, and they were allowed to administer sacraments.

In 1886, when the remains of an 8th century monk were excavated, he was found to be clutching a manuscript, possibly of his favourite book. It was the *Book of Peter*, the original pope, and supposedly contained the real story of the resurrection. This finding caused quite a stir, as outside of cloistered walls, only the approved four Gospels would have been allowed for Church teaching at the time. The manuscript was dated to about AD700, and it cannot be proven whether or not it is a forgery. (Gospels were rarely written personally by the individual whose name they carry; this is not the issue here.) Apparently, the *Gospel of Peter* was referred to in writings of a Turkish bishop around AD190, where his name was invoked for purposes of credibility.

Amongst the Nag Hammadi collection are the full *Gospel of Mary Magdalen*, the *Gospel of Judas* and possibly the best known, the *Gospel of Thomas*, which actually identifies itself as a secret gospel and contains the sentence, "These are the secret words which the living Jesus spoke." Also, "If you bring forth what is within you, what you bring forth will save you. If you do not bring forth what is within you, what you do not bring forth will kill you." Other titles present in the Gnostic texts are the *Apocalypse of James,* the *Apocryphon of John*, *the Gospel of Philip* and the *Gospel of Truth*, to name but a few.

Experts have dated the *Gospel of Thomas* at approximately AD140. (The four New Testament Gospels are dated between AD60 and AD110.) Recently, Professor H. Koetzer of Harvard has suggested that the sayings in Thomas might include even older traditions, possibly even earlier than AD60. This gospel is widely available on YouTube. Fragments of a Greek Gospel of Thomas had been found in 1890, and there was the 8th century monk found in 1886, as mentioned above. The earliest of the four approved Gospels in the New Testament is thought to be Mark, written up to 30 years after the death of Jesus. It is estimated that there were probably about 50 gospels in circulation at the time when the early Christians were being persecuted by the Roman rulers, and many early Christian martyrs were put to death as entertainment for the crowds in countless Roman amphitheatres throughout the Empire.

Amongst the other texts is a very different story of the Garden of Eden, compared to that which we know about from Genesis, which tells it from the point of view of the serpent. There is an extraordinary poem amongst the texts, spoken with the voice of the feminine, including the lines, "I am the wife and the virgin, I am the barren one and many are her sons." The *Gospel of Philip* relates the story of Sophia (See "The Dreaming Goddess" below).

More Secrecy and Suppression

Why were these texts buried, and why has their content remained unknown for nearly two thousand years? The history of Gnosticism represents one of the most suppressed messages ever conceived.

It has been established that while early Christianity was gaining a shaky foothold during the centuries immediately following the crucifixion, so were teachings referred to as gnosis—a Greek word meaning knowledge. These beliefs were at odds with Christianity mainly because no intermediaries were necessary for the followers of Jesus's teachings to find God and presumably eternal life.

The knowledge in question is not rational intelligence, but rather what we might call insight—the process of knowing oneself— and therefore human nature and human destiny. To know oneself at the deepest level is simultaneously to know God, and this is the secret of gnosis. The Gnostics certainly did not consider themselves as heretics, but by the middle of the second century, they had been unequivocally condemned as such by the hierarchy of orthodox Christians who clearly perceived a profound threat to their growing power base. They were condemned by Ignatius of Antioch in AD107; and Bishop Irenaeus, Leader of the Church in Lyon, wrote five volumes criticizing their teachings, referring to these as "madness and blasphemy against God."

By the time of the Emperor Constantine's conversion to Christianity, early in the fourth century, Gnosticism had already been driven firmly underground. Constantine's decision to make Christianity the official religion of the Roman Empire, is largely responsible for its comprehensive spread across the lands around the Mediterranean and much further afield. Possession of books denounced as heretical was made a criminal offence, and any copies found would be burned. Someone, possibly a monk from the nearby monastery of St Pachomius, might have taken the library of texts to Nag Hammadi, where they remained successfully hidden for 1600 years.

The Romans were extraordinarily efficient organisers, and the embers of the Gnostic branch of Christianity were effectively extinguished throughout the Empire. But in Syria, their still extant sacred literatures concerning Thomas are closely related to the Gnostic Gospels. They consider Thomas as the twin of Jesus and guarantor of his wisdom and knowledge. Hermetic literature dating from the first century is named after the Greek god Hermes (nicknamed Trismegistos or Thrice-Great) and follows Gnostic principles. The Mandaeans of Iraq and Iran follow similar teachings, as do the Manichaeans of Europe, the

Middle East, North Africa and China. There are also Islamic Gnostics in the Muslim world.

But when the Cathars of South Western France grew in strength in the thirteenth century, they were seen as such a threat to the Church that extreme measures were undertaken literally to exterminate them. The Cathars were Gnostics who rejected the material world and therefore Catholicism, which had become extremely worldly and which had almost complete authority at the time. The Church was growing in wealth, bureaucracy and power, collecting taxes from all over Europe. The bloody Albigensian Crusade was launched by Pope Innocent III, and killed thousands, particularly in the area of Toulouse, making no distinction between Cathars and anyone else who happened to be in the area. With the Catholic hierarchy not wanting another such heretical menace ever to arise again, the infamous Spanish Inquisition was set up in 1231 and lasted for well over two hundred years.

Gnostics and the Demiurge

Certain Gnostic concepts appear to be unique to them—one concerns a character called the Demiurge, who was inferior to the true God. The true God sent Christ to Earth to save humankind from the evil of the Demiurge.

The Demiurge has various different names, including Yaldabaoth, Samael and Saklas. In Aramaic, Saklas means fool, and Samael means blind god, or god of the blind. Yaldabaoth is harder to translate, but is close to "child of chaos," or even could be a condensed form of "Yahweh, Lord of Sabbaths."

The Aeon Sophia (see "The Dreaming Goddess" section) gave birth to a son who was extraordinarily ugly with the body of a snake and the head of a lion, with "eyes like lightning bolts," according to the *Secret Book of John*. Sophia was deeply horrified at the sight of this offspring, who is named as the Demiurge. She disowned him and cast him out of heaven. In his lonely exile, he created the Archons (this translates as "rulers"), who were beings like him, in order to help him administer the material world, which he then created. This was also chaotic, being a reflection of the personality of its creator.

Next, the Demiurge is said to have created Adam and Eve, and imprisoned divine sparks from heaven within them. He told them he was the only God and issued the Ten Commandments. Jews, Romans, Pagans and fellow Christians found this idea of a creator-god that was demented and essentially a mistake, both shocking and blasphemous.

If we consider a situation where the early Christians were trying to decide on the basics of their new religion, and separate it from Judaism, then this strange Demiurge concept makes a little more sense. The word comes from Plato; he and other philosophers had said that the world was the creation of a divine craftsman. In Judaism, it was established tradition to split off particular faculties of God from God himself, and credit lesser divine beings, such as Wisdom, with having assisted God in the Creation. The Greek word "Logos," which translates as "Word," refers to Jesus Christ, which gives meaning to the beautiful words in the St John Gospel: "In the beginning was the Word, and the Word was with God, and the Word was God ... And the Word was made flesh, and dwelt amongst us."

We might wonder how the Gnostics acquired the idea that the Demiurge was malevolent rather than helpful. It might have been a good faith interpretation of Christian scriptures which were already becoming widespread and popular. This was also the time of the mystery schools, and the concept of many gods (polytheism) was generally held. The idea that only one God should be responsible for everything was probably quite challenging to embrace.

The Mystery Schools of Egypt

These epitomised the ultimate in secret wisdom and knowledge, and it is believed by certain modern scholars and researchers that the great teachers who presided over them had to have come from some extraordinary place. Perhaps they were wise masters who survived the destruction of the lost continent of Atlantis and made their way to the early civilisation of Egypt, where they helped elevate it to a greatness far in advance of other cultures of that era. Some have even suggested that the god Osiris was an extra-terrestrial astronaut from the Pleiades, who first visited Egypt in prehistoric times when it was composed of barbaric tribes. Because he came from an advanced extra-terrestrial culture, say the proponents of this theory, he was considered a god and became the founder of the mystery schools, and raised the primitive Egyptians' standard of living to a remarkable degree.

Even many conservative scholars of the history of religion have a sense that the mystery schools of Egypt contain within their teachings a particular knowledge that came from prehistoric, or at least, ancient times. The earliest legible human records are the Pyramid Texts of Egypt, originating from about 3,000BC. These contain many prayers that are quoted from a far more ancient period, and it is apparent that the prayers were used in the texts as magical formulas and spells.

The mysterious first initiator into these sacred doctrines was known as Toth, later called Hermes by the Greeks. He was the god who delivered messages from the Olympiad, and the god who initiated mortals into transcendent mysteries. Later, the Greek disciples of this secret tradition would call him Hermes Trismegistus (three times great), and he would be credited with originating the material contained in 42 books of esoteric science. To the Romans, Hermes was known as Mercury.

Back in the time of the Rameses, 1300 BC, seekers of the divine sciences came from distant Asia Minor and Greece to study in the sanctuaries with magi and hierophants, who they believed could give them the secrets of immortality. The students, who would become initiates of the mystery schools, had to undertake the rigors of disciplined study and the training of body, mind and spirit, involving a complete restructuring of their physical, moral and spiritual being. Only by developing one's faculties of will, intuition and reason to an extraordinary degree, could one ever gain access to the hidden forces in the Universe. Through complete mastery of body, mind and spirit, they could see beyond death and perceive the pathways to be taken in the afterlife. Having conquered fate and acquired divine freedom, the initiate—who could be male or female—became a seer, a magician, an initiator. The seven Hermetic Principles may be found in the *Kybalion.*

Around 550 BC, the Greek philosopher **Pythagoras** learned the secret doctrine of numbers, the heliocentric system of the Universe, music, astrology, astronomy, mathematics and geometry, from the powerful Egyptian magi. Before he established his own school of philosophy in southern Italy, Pythagoras spent 22 years in the temples of Egypt as an initiate in the ancient mysteries. For centuries, the pharaohs themselves were the pupils and instruments of the hierophants and the magicians, who presided over the temples and cults of **Isis** and **Osiris.** Each pharaoh received his initiation name from the temple, and the priests were honoured with the roles of counsellors and advisors to the throne. Some have even referred to the rule of ancient Egypt as government of the initiates.

Although the ancient Egyptians never appeared to produce a philosophical system in the manner of the Greeks or the Romans, the mysteries produced a remarkable number of systematised theologies that dealt with the essential questions about the true nature of humankind and its relationship to the cosmos. The hierophants created theological constructs and formulated esoteric answers that brought initiates and aspirants to the great religious cities of Heliopolis, Memphis, Hermopolis Magna, Abydos and Thebes.

The Dreaming Goddess

John Lamb Lash, who is probably the most knowledgeable authority on Sophia, the Wisdom Goddess, has made it his life's work to interpret the most difficult and fragmented Nag Hammadi translations. *The Gospel of Philip* tells the following story, which was unknown before the Nag Hammadi translations: In the Gnostic mythical tradition, heaven was referred to as the "Pleroma" or fullness, located in the centre of our galaxy, where gods and goddesses (for which the Gnostic word is Aeon) existed. In the beginning, there were no planets or stars in the core. The Aeons spent their existences dreaming and concocting experiments, in a raw matrix of divine living light, within huge currents of swirling energy. A male and female Aeon collaborated on a DNA plasma, and the human species was created. (There is a Hindu myth that this DNA is experimental, badly designed and has destroyed itself, on nine previous occasions. The DNA plasma is like a highly gifted child with extreme capacities and which cannot handle its own power.)

Sophia (the Greek word for wisdom) was a young Aeon, a creative but impulsive galactic being, who became very concerned and wanted to rectify the situation. Unable to obtain permission from God, she tried to conceive on her own, without the involvement of her heavenly partner. The resulting child that she produced was the Demiurge, a son who was horribly deformed, because he was the product of the "rebellious and profane desire" that had arisen within her. She had crossed a boundary, and her disgrace had caught up with her. She banished this son, and she herself fell into the galaxy. Sophia became the Earth. This myth is unique to Gnosticism.

As a result of her fall, chaos ensued and, in his boredom, the banished Demiurge created the Archons. They have been called our freak cosmic cousins, these accidental by-products of Sophia's fall. An Archon is not human but has the power to take over the human mind. The translation of the *Apocryphon of John* says that she committed adultery with the Archons, but **Lash** disputes this—he says she became adulterated by them and became the Earth. The Archons have a hive mentality and are inorganic, producing the inorganic part of our solar system: everything but the sun, moon and Earth. The Archons became aware of the uniqueness of planet Earth, and exhibiting extreme jealousy, they infested it. This presents a huge problem for us, and is coming to a head in the present times. **Lash** points to a correction being under way, and identifies disasters such as Fukushima as representing part of the correction manifesting.

Much more detail on this subject, and speculation on what is likely to be in store as the "correction" progresses, is set out in **Lash's** book *Not in His Image.*

Mother Nature

The beautiful and well-known domed church in Istanbul, known as Hagia Sophia, has made Sophia's name famous. But it was built in the 6th century by the Eastern Christians of Constantinople, and was dedicated (it was claimed by the Romans) to a minor virgin martyr, Saint Sophia, rather than built in honour of any feminine divinity.

Hagia means "holy" in Greek and was also once a term of respect for a wise, older woman. Sadly, it's also the original root of the word "hag," which is used as a derogatory term for any woman. The historical inferiority of women and the suppression of the goddess are related, just as the dominance of men is related to monotheism. As the knowledge of the feminine divinity disappeared, the patriarchy—which is based upon negating women's spiritual authority—flourished. Over time, the Bible was altered constantly, and as there is no word for goddess in Hebrew, there were never any mentions of women in positions of power. When the Bible mentions Yahweh's abolition of false gods, this refers apparently to the eradication of goddess worship. The Promised Land, Canaan, was already occupied by a goddess-worshipping people, and after that land had been conquered, prophets spoke against Asherah, Anath and Ashtoreth, who were female divinities! Asherah was the Semitic name of the great goddess, the "Mother of all Wisdom."

The religious roles of priest, pastor or rabbi were not held by women until the end of the twentieth century. They were simply not allowed to fulfil any inner calling to mediate between divinity and a congregation. The Catholic Church, Orthodox Judaism and the Baptists still will not acknowledge the equality of women. In times past, the only place for a woman seeking mystical union with God was in a convent, or community of women mystics. Often, if women spoke openly of mystical experiences or spiritual revelations, this could have led to being diagnosed as delusional, and being committed to some sort of asylum. St Joan of Arc, who heard voices that allowed her to guide the French army to victory, was burned at the stake as a witch. Church authorities so feared her that the outcome of her trial for heresy was a foregone conclusion.

Every ancient culture has had its version of the Earth Goddess. The Greeks called her Gaia; and to the Incas, she was Pachamama. Ancient shrines, long pre-dating language, paintings and statues of her have been found in all corners of the world. She is life, the very soul of the planet. Today, we are familiar with the term Mother Nature. Gaia was considered the primeval mother, from whom all gods—and life itself—descended. Interest in Gaia has been reignited with the rise of New Age practices over the last half-century or so. There is a new understanding growing of just how our planet operates. In 1970, **James Lovelock** and his research partner, **Lynn Margulis** (wife of **Carl Sagan** at the time), proposed that the Earth is a living being, which self-regulates the elements in order to sustain life upon itself. Their theory suggests that chemicals in the Earth "talk" to one another and work in harmony to protect Earth's creatures. The story of Sophia, who fell into the Earth and became the Earth, is the Gnostic version of the story of Mother Nature.

The previous chapters have discussed religion, spirituality, truth, conspiracy and suppression. These diverse but related themes provide a background for the strange times in which we find ourselves living today. A well-known Chinese curse is the title of the next chapter, which details some of the more pressing issues through which all of us on the planet are navigating.

Chapter 5

"May You Live in Interesting Times"

"I've come to believe that all my past failure and frustration were actually laying the foundation for the understandings that have created the new level of living I now enjoy."
Tony Robbins

Conspiracy and Communism

Did you know that in Germany, the term "Nazi" was an abbreviation for National Socialism? And that Communism is International Revolutionary Socialism? Powerful people have, since the beginning, sought to gain mastery over others. In the USA, the Founding Fathers recognised the principles of socialism as a deadly threat to the inalienable rights of life, liberty, property and the pursuit of happiness, and attempted to make its principles unconstitutional. Behind the Iron Curtain, populations of numerous European countries suffered economic hardship and political oppression whilst just a few at the top grew rich. **George Orwell's** polemic *Animal Farm* is an allegorical story of communism (and human society), where the animals overthrow their cruel and oppressive human masters, hoping to live in freedom and comfort. By the end of the novella, all are under the iron fist of the ruthless pigs, self-elected leaders who tell them "all animals might be equal, but some are more equal than others."

I will be using the terms socialism and communism inter-changeably, because whilst this might be a little inaccurate, no distinction is necessary here. Successive governments in the US have been alert to the threat of infiltration by communism. **Joseph McCarthy** was an attorney, and a Republican senator, who from 1950 became the most public face of the war against communist subversion. He gave his name to McCarthyism, a term used today more broadly to mean demagogic, reckless, and unsubstantiated accusations, as well as public attacks on the character or patriotism of political opponents. "Reds under the bed" gives an idea of how the witch-hunt is perceived now, and by many at the time. **Arthur Miller's** play *The Crucible* (1953) was allegorical, based on the Salem witch trials, but was clearly a commentary on the McCarthyism of the time.

The unfortunate facts are that the socialists have largely succeeded in their aims. Patience is an integral part of their strategy—they acted slowly and imperceptibly, working on the minds of the population, particularly the young, encouraging well-meaning citizens to accept their superficial slogans.

When the Soviet Union fell in 1989, the communists merely changed their tactics. While the West assumed victory, they never accepted defeat. Working with **J Edgar Hoover** of the FBI, in 1963, **Dr W. Cleon Skousen** identified 45 *"Current Socialist Goals."* Many of these are specific to America, and the full list is easily found on the internet. I am not going to list them all here, but I find their following successes and works-in-progress worth mentioning:

- Do away with oaths of loyalty;
- Get control of schools; soften the curriculum;
- Gain control of student newspapers;
- Gain control of key positions in radio, television and motion pictures;
- Control art critics and museums...foster a cult of ugly, meaningless and repulsive art;
- Eliminate obscenity laws, calling them censorship, or violation of free speech;
- Infiltrate churches...discredit the Bible...emphasise intellectual maturity as not needing a "crutch";
- Present homosexuality, degeneracy and promiscuity as "normal, natural and healthy";
- Discredit the American Founding Fathers. Present them as selfish aristocrats, with no concern for the "common man";
- Support movements that give centralised control over education, social agencies, welfare programs, mental health clinics, etc.;
- Infiltrate and gain control of unions;
- Transfer certain powers of arrest from the police to social agencies. Categorise behavioural problems as psychiatric disorders which only psychiatrists can understand or treat;
- Discredit the family as an institution. Encourage promiscuity and easy divorce;
- Overthrow all colonial governments before native populations are ready for self-government.

Organised Chaos

The advances in technology over the last half-century are astounding, and we are enthusiastically embracing this in all forms. There are unsettling side effects, however, as it becomes an integral part of our lives. We are dependent upon electricity like never before; and keeping up with developments, simply in order to not be left behind, requires investment of both time and money. The young in particular are being targeted. They hardly talk to each other—they are continually using their phones, not to speak but to have conversations via text, to take and send pictures or to play games. Smartphone addiction is a real thing. It isn't only children who can't bear to be parted from their phones—and what possesses people to line up for hours in the middle of the night to purchase the newest model of the iPhone or whatever?

Audible and visible alerts from dozens of apps break concentration. Productivity in the workplace, apparently, has stagnated in the last decade rather than advanced, and this is blamed on the levels of distraction arising from constant interruption by technology. It can take a full fifteen minutes to regain maximum concentration after being jerked out of it by a bell, or an onscreen message—and many of us don't even attempt to ignore these, but automatically spend time investigating the details there and then.

Consider the smart technology that is increasingly present in our homes. Not only computers and television sets that have remarkable capabilities, but voice controlled equipment that plays music, reminds us to do things, or which we can consult if we want to learn, for example, whether a particular store is open or what the state of traffic flow is in a nearby town. Our homes are full of "stuff," much of which is being sold to us under the cloak of convenience. The rapidly developing "internet of things"—which will incorporate a step further than the chip and pin in our credit cards—involves having RFID chips implanted in the body. Walk towards your locked front door and it opens; say the word and the blinds come down or the lights come on; you talk to your equipment; your fridge refills itself; your car drives itself—yes indeed, it's convenient, but soon we will not have to move to do anything! Obesity, incidentally, is becoming a major concern to many governments, and there will be much more detail about this in Chapter 9.

Regarding these implants, my instinct is to resist, and firmly. RFID stands for Radio Frequency Identification. Consider the freedoms that will be sacrificed. Our every action can be tracked. Big Brother will know all there is to know about us. You will be aware that I am referring to *Nineteen Eighty Four*, but you might not have read it. I re-read it only last year and recognised just how chilling and predictive this book was—**George Orwell** just got the date wrong.

Google and Facebook are at the cutting edge of this advancing technology. These behemoths know more about us, and our habits, than we do ourselves. Amazon's Jeff Bezos, for several years the richest man in the world, has become the planet's first multi-trillionaire, largely as a result of the pandemic and worldwide lockdowns. There is an Agenda here.

Increasingly present in our lives is AI: artificial intelligence. Again in the name of convenience, a dream is being sold to us. Younger people are particularly vulnerable to the sales pitch... "Connect to AI and you will become superhuman." Or will they become sub-human, controlled by AI, because whoever controls AI will be controlling them... Might we all be sleepwalking into a trap?

Which leads me back to the subject of 5th generation wireless communication (5G) about which so little is heard in mainstream media. This is no accident; but we need to question why there has been a news blackout on this sensitive subject for several years. Naturally, we turn to alternative media, and learn that 5G is very frightening indeed. Again, it's something being introduced under the guise of convenience: ultra-fast downloads—a whole box set dealt with in seconds! We will need it for driverless cars, in themselves an amazing concept, and for the internet of things.

But 5G is microwave technology, involving the use of high frequency millimetre waves. The concern is that it hasn't been tested for safety, it is being introduced far too fast and no debate is being allowed. If Rent-a-Mob knew more, they would be holding protests on a regular basis, because 5G will be a live biological experiment on humanity. 5G technology is currently in use for crowd control in the third world—the same way water cannons were once employed—and it works by causing a very unpleasant burning sensation on the skin, causing crowds to disperse at speed. The risks of 5G are far greater than politics and security.

Herd Immunity, Isolation and Imprisonment

From time to time, medical experts recount the virtues of "herd immunity" for diseases such as measles, and maintain that this is the best way to keep a population safe from a particular threat. Usually they are recommending use of a vaccination, in itself controversial, but the idea is, broadly, that the more people who have developed immunity from a particular pathogen, the less likely that unprotected members of the population will catch it.

It might go without saying that there are better ways than vaccination to develop immunity, such as diet and cleanliness, of which more detail is in Chapter 9. But the one advantage that vaccination delivers is speed, which is why it is being hailed as the answer to the COVID-19 spread.

The UK government has denied that herd immunity was ever part of its developing COVID policy last year, although it was certainly being discussed by scientists at the time. Eventually, the declared strategy became protection of the most vulnerable, and protection of the NHS through containment, delay, research and mitigation of the effects of the pandemic. Herd immunity inevitably develops *after* epidemics, but clearly the time delay was assessed as unacceptable. It is necessary for up to 90% of a population to develop this immunity, and since COVID-19 was a completely new virus, no one at all had protection at the start.

A report by **Professor Neil Ferguson** (Professor Panic, or Professor Lockdown) warned that the UK was on track for 250,000 deaths unless stringent and immediate remedial measures were taken, and policy makers were unnerved. And so lockdown was declared, in the wake of procedures followed in Italy, the first European country to be hard hit by the virus, and China. In China, people are seen merely as tools of collective national policy, but in a democracy, it is supposed to be different.

Locking up healthy people has never before been considered—it was usual to isolate those who are ill or in quarantine—and yet we all quietly accepted it. There is no question that the majority were driven by fear, and this was massaged and developed by news broadcasts and special COVID-19 broadcasts provided for daily consumption.

Our status as a free society depends on convention, a collective instruction as to the right way to behave. In the UK, policing operated by consent. It used to be accepted that there were certain things a democratic government could not do, and until March 2020, one of these was locking up healthy people in their own homes. The Civil Contingencies Act was hurriedly passed, giving our government the ability to do anything an Act of Parliament can do—without the normal debate and safeguards. The police, in particular, were given wide ranging powers, and although actions taken under the above Act require parliamentary consent within 7 days, this was considered as being practically a foregone conclusion. Convention, which we have now cast aside, used to be our protection from such laws.

Instant Gratification

Previous generations used to save up for things—this was normal practice and good training for their offspring. By the time enough had been accumulated to buy the object in question, either one was absolutely sure of the need for it, or else the desire had worn off with the passage of time. So no money would be wasted. Hire purchase was not society's first introduction to the concept of "have now, pay later," but perhaps it was the new, socially acceptable face of debt. My parents always treated the idea with great scepticism—in their eyes it still amounted to being in debt, which was quite simply a disgrace, proof that one could not manage one's finances.

With the introduction of credit cards, temptation has escalated. So much more is now within reach, and it isn't even necessary to enter into formal repayment agreements each time we borrow for the sake of acquiring something we cannot quite afford. However, these cards are dangerous weapons, there for the purpose of controlling us, because once we get into serious credit card debt, it is extremely difficult to get out. Why do we give into temptation? It is the appeal of having something right now, without waiting, just because we have the choice.

The credit companies want us to take advantage of the minimum payment arrangements that they offer, and not to pay attention to the size of the debt. Depending on the percentage interest charged by the company, the debt can grow at an alarming rate as interest is charged on interest. Credit cards, skilfully used, are a great innovation, but discipline is required. Generally speaking, we should aim to pay each one off at the end of the month, whenever this is possible. We need to stop spending, before the outstanding balance gets out of hand.

Many have been advised to cut up their credit cards, once their spending habits have been recognised as a problem. Bear in mind, though, that there is an additional challenge when it comes to ordering online—not only will many sites offer to store your card details, so that you simply pay by pressing a single button, but often your browser also saves the information! If resisting temptation is too much of a challenge, it is recommended to take steps to remove card details from all memories.

Dieters struggle to resist sugar, in all its many forms; giving into sweet temptation is just another angle to the instant gratification problem. Beware, substituting calorie-free sweet drinks does more harm than good, because if your taste buds keep relishing the taste that they love, the sweet habit is only strengthened. Some of the chemical sweeteners are poisons, but it takes years to prove allegations and have them removed from production. Many people give up sugar in tea and coffee for Lent, or as a New Year's resolution, and find that the beverages actually taste better unsweetened. It is possible to transfer this preference to other food and drink over time, with just a little perseverance.

Many keep their cupboards sweet free (that is, no biscuits, chocolates, preserves and so on) because it is easier to stay on track if temptation is removed. For those with a weight problem, if you know you can't resist something, because instant gratification feels so good, then make sure you stay out of temptation's way. The same applies to alcohol and gambling, which are all forms of dependence or addiction—that is, simply, the inability to resist instant gratification.

Social media has absolutely tapped into humanity's love of this sort of pleasure. The concept of gathering "likes" on Facebook, or "views" on YouTube, can easily become an obsession. A tiny dopamine "hit" is achieved every time the totals increase. Lack of these little marks of appreciation actually causes disappoint-ment, frustration, or worse. The hold that these social media platforms have over so many people is having an impact on society. At the very least, it can be an immeasurable waste of time; as a distraction, it is having a serious effect on concentration and productivity. Role models, or influencers, have made huge fortunes by seizing an opportunity at just the right time, but this will not happen for the majority.

It isn't even enough to be visible on one or two platforms, we are told, as presence is required on an ever-increasing number of them. The series of lockdowns we have been living with have acclimatised everyone to interacting less and less with their fellow human beings, but social media is playing its part. Even beforehand, it was noticeable at social gatherings and business meetings that during breaks, people would be busily tapping away on their phones, or scrolling through content and messages, rather than actually talking to each other.

The Great Reset

In 1699, the Royal Mint had a very serious problem. A massive amount of the currency in use—10% of all coins in circulation—were known to be fake. **Isaac Newton**, a visionary with a brilliant mind and an extensive knowledge of mathematics, was appointed Warden of the Mint and charged with bringing order to the chaos of Britain's financial system. His stringent reforms were said to have flushed the system and made our money work again. This was the first reset.

Right now we are at another historic turning point. There is about to be another re-coinage even more radical than **Newton's**. Old money will die. In October 2020, IMF Managing Director **Christina Georgieva** said, "We face a new Bretton Woods moment." She referred to the famous meeting of 1944, whose purpose was to construct a new global monetary system, the second reset.

For some years, at least since the global crash of 2008, central banks all over the world have been devaluing their national currencies in order to pay down their enormous debts. The ordinary consumer suffers because any saved money loses its value. Almost imperceptibly, the historically low pound, combined with low interest rates and creeping inflation, have sucked the lifeblood out of our finances.

Add to this the global financial shutdown initiated by the panic of COVID-19, and we can see March 2020 as a proverbial line in the sand. Central banks worldwide ramped up money printing to unbelievable levels on the basis that it was the only way they could see to keep economies running. For the first time in history, six of the world's largest economies flooded the world with a deluge of printed money. Indisputably, the financial system is once again totally corrupted and broken.

According to data from 2015, police in the USA seize more cash from private citizens than criminals steal. In that same year, the chief economist at the Bank of England proposed a complete ban on cash. Between November 2017 and November 2019, cash points in the UK vanished at an average rate of 300 every single month. It is illegal for French citizens to pay for anything over €1,000 in cash. Cash payments cannot be taxed, because they are invisible. Governments hate cash and are acting to stop us from using it—in Sweden, it's more expensive to pay with cash than with plastic. Since lockdown, the majority of businesses in the UK have insisted on payment via plastic, and we must wonder whether cash will ever become universally accepted again.

Banks will tell us how expensive it is to handle money. But it's also very expensive to handle cards. Handling fees are always built into prices, regardless of payment method. Visa, MasterCard and PayPal generate €1 trillion per year in fees—a veritable goldmine for the banks.

For years, we have been encouraged to tap our little pieces of plastic in the shops—but at least we used to have a choice! We are falling in line with the "Plan" because it's so convenient; but a significant result is that it's that much harder to keep control of what we are spending.

Certain governments are on the cusp of a roll out of Central Bank digital currencies (CBDCs). This has nothing whatever to do with cryptocurrencies, which are decentralised. With CBDCs, there will be a mass centralisation of power into the hands of the central banks, who will force us to use a digital currency issued by them directly into our accounts. So the Central Bank will be in control of our wealth, paving the way for a whole new level of surveillance and overreach of authority.

Most will recognise in this the potential end of cash, but it gets worse: They could put a "timer" on our savings, forcing us to spend 30% or 40% of our money (before it disappears) whenever it suits them. Or they could implement different interest rates for different groups of people—generous rates for those they want to please, and negative rates for those whose votes don't matter.

Consider the spectre of social credit scores, where your bank account is interlinked with your legal, employment and medical history, your marital status and even your web history! Sounds too dystopian? It's already in use today in China; and currently, 100 million people are excluded from using the public transport system to fly across the country—they have no means of payment. And China has launched trials of CBDC in 4 of its cities. So will we have to choose between participating in a system that would enforce restraints on our privacy and liberty, or taking out at least some capital and still being a part of the rise of the new money?

Cryptocurrency will be outside the reach of governmental interference. It used to be said that gold was where the smart money went in uncertain times, and to an extent this was true recently while its value rose steadily as the pandemic progressed. But strangely, so did the value of stocks, because these were being artificially supported. Money now seems to be moving out of gold, and the chances are that investors are purchasing cryptocurrencies in response to a financial system that is rigged and distorted almost beyond meaning. The gains could be astronomical—and once again, the biggest of these will go to those able to take advantage with their already huge fortunes.

The Unseen Enemy

In 1815, there was a gigantic volcanic explosion at Mount Tambora in Indonesia, and the air was choked with ash and dust. About a hundred thousand people died in the immediate vicinity, but the eventual death toll was massively higher than this. Debris filled the air, blocking the sun, and was carried by air currents all around the northern hemisphere. The next summer simply never arrived. Most of Europe was covered in unrelenting fog and frost. Famously, this was the summer of darkness, when **Mary Shelly** wrote *Frankenstein*, whilst on holiday at Lake Geneva with poet **Percy Bysshe Shelly** and **Lord Byron**. All that concerned them was finding diversions with which to pass the time during their annual lakeside holiday, which this year had been wrecked by wind, cold and rain.

The darkness lasted three years, causing famines, epidemics and political revolts. Tens of millions died from a global cholera pandemic that resulted from the general mayhem. We can imagine how it must have felt during those three cold years— plenty must have thought that the end of the world was upon them. But gradually the air cleared, the sun's rays warmed the Earth again and normal life resumed.

There was another worldwide pandemic in 1918, just as the Great War was finally coming to an end. This was the Spanish Flu, the influenza outbreak that killed between 30 and 50 million victims. The first wave, in the summer of that year, was mild and most recovered, but the second wave, which followed in the autumn, was lethal. Victims died within days, sometimes hours of falling ill. Unexpectedly, the young and healthy were badly afflicted, and more US soldiers died from the flu than were killed in battle during the war. It was a worldwide pandemic, but records at the time in many places were non-existent. Some estimates of the death toll run as high as one hundred million, worldwide, which equates to 3% of the world's population. There was a third wave, in 1919, and a fourth, comparatively minor one in 1920.

The disease did not originate in Spain, but that country was hard hit whilst not under the typical wartime news blackouts that affected most European countries. So Spain is where news coverage originated. Internationally, the authorities had no idea how to cope with the situation, which was exacerbated by lack of medical personnel due to deaths during the war. Cities closed saloons and theatres only after death rates were already alarmingly high, and only then did citizens have to wear masks in public on pain of a $5 fine—a large sum of money at the time. The Spanish Flu was known as the "forgotten pandemic"—at least, it was one of several named as such—until COVID-19 struck the world last year. Everybody knows about the 1918 outbreak now, and frequent comparisons are made. "There's nothing new under the sun," the sages might tell us; and indeed, governments had apparently been planning for another flu outbreak for many years. Not well enough, evidently.

Right at the start of the COVID-19 panic, you could find reports on YouTube (not mainstream news, obviously) of a simulation exercise carried out close to Wuhan in China, involving American soldiers. There just happens to be a research lab on the outskirts of that city, where lethal diseases, specifically those caused by alteration of naturally occurring viruses, are studied. A moratorium on such activity in the USA was decreed in 2014, after numerous disconcerting accidents resulting from carelessness with smallpox, influenza and anthrax viruses. Experimentation in weaponising infectious diseases was the reason for the research, which was still considered vital. A certain Dr Anthony Fauci directed that the American funding simply be diverted to Wuhan, and the laboratory there was licenced accordingly.

So, the above "war games" scenario, plausibly, was responsible for the virus moving from a laboratory to a bat or to a pangolin, or some species in a wet market, and from there to humans. Only the final piece of the story was well circulated. And whatever planning might have been done by governments internationally, it was clearly not sufficient to deal with the real thing. We heard the words "unprecedented" and "incredibly" numerous times per broadcast as leaders gnashed their teeth and stared at the oncoming headlights. The one thing, strangely, that governments worldwide seemed to agree upon, was to crash their economies. Countless businesses were ordered to close; some owners were compensated, and many were not.

Eventually we were all put under house arrest, and ordered to wear masks if we ventured into contact with other people. Christmas was cancelled, amidst great disappointment, and then at the last minute, in the UK, schools were again shut as the second wave got fully under way.

Unlike in 1918, scientists have been able to produce a vaccination, at breakneck speed and apparently without observation of what used to be considered essential safety testing. That, together with herd immunity, should allow everyone to have a half-decent summer. We will all wait with interest to find out how long it will be before we are allowed to pursue the pleasures we used to take for granted, like saunas, massages and overseas travel.

Vaccination theory, of course, has considerable controversy attached to it. Our bodies were designed to heal themselves, and we are born with powerful but immature immune systems. Together with mothers' milk and the right environment, infants are able to fight off common infections. But as we grow, we learn to reach for over-the-counter remedies or seek medical help for most issues. In the following chapters, these matters will receive further discussion, and to begin with, I will be considering the importance of energy.

Chapter 6

Vibration and Healing

"Fear, conformity, immorality: these are heavy burdens. They drain us of creative energy. And when we are drained of creative energy, we do not create. We procreate, but we do not create."
David McCallum

Attraction and Resonance

Do you remember, as a child, using a magnifying glass to light a campfire, or maybe playing with one, directing the sun's rays onto a piece of wood, then burning a pattern or perhaps your name onto it? This burning can only be achieved by concentrating the energy of the sun right down into a tiny dot—and the same principle applies when setting and working towards a goal: Energy flows where focus goes. And of course, in order to focus, we need to know exactly what we want.

Not approximately or vaguely, but in detail. This could come as a surprise, but the concept of identifying exactly what we want is not as simple as it sounds. A better job, more money and less aggravation are not exact instructions! It is necessary to rephrase, in terms of naming the job or promotion that you have in mind; put a figure on the monthly or annual salary that you want, and define precisely what "less aggravation" means in your life.

Goal setting is a very exact science; not only must we decide what we want, but we must be able to describe it in detail. We use the acronym SMART (specific, measurable, achievable, realistic and timebound) to help with the description. The goal must be written down and referred back to frequently—possibly even daily. Some check their goals in the morning and evening to keep them uppermost in their minds. **Raymond Aaron** has an improvement on the goal setting process: Having chosen and described your goal, write down 3 versions of it, with the middle one being the outcome you genuinely think you can achieve in the time available. He calls the levels MTO (being minimum, target and outrageous), and I really recommend the upgrade—it works!

So, you keep thinking about these goals, and it's like putting in an order to the Universe. **Michael Beckwith** says that a positive thought is 100 times more powerful than a negative one (very positive thinking!) Our thoughts act as magnets. All inventions started off in someone's mind ("thoughts become things"), and thoughts have a frequency. So, you can think of the Law of Attraction as the Law of Resonance. You will attract vibrations that resonate with your thoughts—that's how it works.

Musicians, as they use tuning forks, are tapping into resonance as they enable their instrument to produce exactly the right tone. When you hear orchestras tune up before a performance, they are confirming that each individual instrument will be playing in harmony with all the others. Failure to carry out this step will ruin the sound of the ensemble.

This Law of Resonance is important in more circumstances than just goal setting and music. The life we experience has been called an out-picturing of what is going on in our heads. So address your thoughts and preferences, and take care what you read or watch on television, what films you see or what video games you play. Notice how music affects your mood, and use it when you feel the urge for a positivity boost! Keep your workspace tidy and organised if you want to be able to think clearly and manage overwhelm. Remove clutter from your surroundings in order to allow the *chi*, or energy, to flow freely and keep you inspired. This last suggestion is a principle of feng shui.

Also do not forget that negative thoughts have huge power (**Michael Beckwith's** comments notwithstanding!). We need to be aware that sometimes these are operating from deep within our subconscious and can cancel out the positive thoughts intentionally directed towards those goals. **Bob Proctor** describes this situation as the paradigm. It is the result of the subconscious programming to which we have been exposed since birth (if not before!), and it drives the way we do everything.

In addition, past experiences can have such a profound effect on our subconscious that it firmly holds us back from realising the achievements we pursue. The oldest part of our brain—the reptile brain—which is in charge of keeping us safe, can at times be overzealous in identifying potential dangers. Some call this "subconscious interference"; some use the term "limiting beliefs." I will discuss methods of dealing with these issues, in Chapter 7.

What Is the Secret?

Most probably you have noticed that when you are in a bad mood, things keep happening to make you feel even worse. You might wake up late, have to leave the house in a hurry, discover that you haven't charged your phone, miss your train, break something, and then have an argument with the next person you see. Several or all of these things happening in succession just compound the original problem. Maybe one of the earliest questions I learnt was, "Did you get out of bed on the wrong side this morning?"

Being a literal person, even then as a child, I pointed out that this wasn't possible considering the location of my bed; so the expression was explained in terms of my being grumpy or miserable. As we grow older, we recognise what seems like the inevitability of bad luck, and there are all sorts of superstitions around, such as walking under a ladder bringing bad luck, breaking a mirror (that one gives you 7 years' worth), avoiding the number 13, and magpies best being seen in pairs.

There are countless others, and we should banish them from our thought processes immediately! The problem being that if we expect bad luck, that's exactly what we will get. Our thoughts act as powerful magnets and, in due course, what we think about becomes our reality.

Very frequently, right from our earliest years, we may be trained to "make the best of things"—in other words, not to expect good fortune as something that is equally as likely as bad fortune. But what if you are simply having "one of those days"? Why do we believe in these things? A day is just a day. And it's up to us to choose what we do with it.

Numerous psychological studies have proved that people generally will invest upwards of 10 times more energy, and even money, into avoiding pain rather than pursuing pleasure! Why? If the two are evenly possible, then this makes no sense at all.

Norman Vincent Peale wrote the *Power of Positive Thinking*, back in 1952. Probably the first of the personal development (PD) writers to focus on the idea of expectation, the book had a remarkable effect at the time and was still being quoted by my dad decades after he had read it. My mum hadn't found it particularly convincing, but I guess she was a natural worrier. Maybe that's the way with mothers—they can't help practicing negative risk assessment on behalf of their offspring! But they would do better to change this thinking and also, when issuing warnings, take care to express these in the positive: "Be careful up there" rather than "Don't fall!"

Some 25 years prior to the above publication, **Napoleon Hill** published *Think and Grow Rich*, which is still considered foundational in terms of PD. The language is slightly more old-fashioned and the book therefore a little harder to read, but it's still recommended by almost all PD trainers. However, it is possible that a great many modern readers do not pick out some of the magic contained in its pages, as we tend, these days, to be impatient and in pursuit of a quick fix.

In 2006, **Rhonda Byrne** published her famous book *The Secret*, and it was made into an enormously successful film the same year. She credits **Wallace D Wattles'** book, *The Science of Getting Rich,* as containing the secret which caused her epiphany, but I don't think that book says anything different to **Napoleon Hill's**. The language is even harder to digest... and it's possible to get to the end of the book without identifying the secret that he admits is hidden within.

Just in case this and the previous section haven't given it away, YOU are the secret! You are responsible for how you think and for every choice you make. Life is all about choice. Never say "I want" but rather "I choose." And it is essential to expect the outcome that you have chosen. This is what is meant by creatorship.

Choice, Ownership and Belief

Life doesn't just happen. Events do not unfold of their own accord—they occur because at some point we have set up certain pathways. If this has not been done intentionally—that is, with the conscious mind—the power of the subconscious comes into play. We have been told that we make our own luck. In this chapter, which introduces ownership, I will not discuss those severe life challenges that might cause you to exclaim, "How could anyone possibly choose *that* (circumstance or disability)?" But I will address this later, in Chapter 7, and there was a hint in Chapter 1.

Not only do we have to choose those positive events or outcomes, we have to expect that they will happen. We must believe that events will conjoin to bring about the results we have ordered—**Michael Beckwith** talks about the "Benevolent Universe." Ownership means that we must be comfortable with taking responsibility for the outcomes of our actions (and thoughts!) This means not leaving developments to an external force: to fate or to fortune, or "letting the Universe decide." There is nothing wrong with surrendering to God, or the Force or the Universe, as far as the HOW is concerned—that is, the method in which your result will be obtained... but the choice about the WHAT is absolutely down to you.

The power of the subconscious mind is remarkably strong. All of us know about the placebo effect: In countless, proven trials (and real-life examples), sugar pills work as well as real medicine. This is not, as I originally thought, because the patient was suffering from an imaginary issue. It is a question of how much faith the patient's subconscious has in the power of the treatment being administered.

Remarkable situations and experiments have been documented which prove the effect of belief, even where cancer or surgery had been involved. A skilled surgeon completed a study on patients with arthritic knees, who were scheduled for operations. On half of the patients, the surgical procedure was carried out, under general anaesthetic of course. The other half believed that the surgery had been undertaken on their own knees, but in fact, all that had actually happened was that a couple of incisions were made, the knees bandaged up and immobilised as with the real operation, and all aspects of aftercare were the same. Recovery rates showed no difference between the two groups of patients!

A patient dying from a rare form of cancer begged to be allowed to participate in a trial being run to test the safety of a new drug. After being accepted, his tumour stopped growing and, after a short time, he went into full remission. For a while, everyone, including the patient, thought that a miracle cure had been found, and his health went from strength to strength. Unfortunately, other patients did not show such dramatic improvements, and an article appeared in a national newspaper saying that the trial was going very badly and that it looked like this new drug would prove to be completely ineffective.

Our patient read the article, his recovery immediately reversed and, within a short time, he was back in his doctor's consulting room. Somehow the doctor managed to convince him that the article was wrong, and that in certain circumstances, including those which, happily, applied to the man himself, the drug was indeed effective. As before, the man went through a seemingly miraculous cure, until some months later he saw another article, which declared the new wonder drug had proved to be a total failure. Sadly, this time his health declined so rapidly that he died shortly afterwards.

Both of these stories are related by **Jose Silva** in his *Mind Control* books and courses, and they demonstrate the amazing power of the subconscious in the area of belief. This power of belief, together with a fertile imagination, has allowed numerous well-known personalities to realise extraordinary successes. As **Napoleon Hill** reminds us in the famous *Think and Grow Rich*, "Whatever the mind can conceive and believe, it can achieve."

Everything Is Energy

Our bodies are made of compressed energy, and even things that we perceive as solid and inorganic are vibrating at a measurable rate. Clearly the vibrations of something dead are minimal and very hard to detect, but without wishing to become too graphic, we know that decomposition will eventually occur—"dust to dust" and all that. Spirits vibrate very, very fast, which to some extent explains why they are invisible to our human senses.

Successful people vibrate faster and feel happier. Around them, things happen. Their own high levels of vibration cause others around them to vibrate in harmony. These folk have accessed their inner power and are using tools available to all of us, as they continue to progress and accomplish their goals. They acknowledge the importance of recognising what they already have, and also expressing gratitude for what they still expect to achieve. Daily journalling is a popular habit, often practiced first thing in the morning, because they find that starting the day with a positive mental attitude sets them up for tackling difficult issues later on in the day.

Happiness is contagious—it's up there along with the other top vibrations: enthusiasm, compassion, gratitude, love and joy. We're all familiar with the lift in mood that comes from spending time with someone who is truly positive. The company we keep has a dramatic effect on our psyches. As we raise our vibrations, we enjoy better overall health, improved sleep, happier relationships and increased productivity. Happiness breeds happiness; positivity breeds positivity. What we perceive in our external circumstances is a direct reflection of what we are inside.

When working towards success in any new venture, it's essential to believe that it is possible and that it WILL happen. We learn that we should see ourselves as happy, or successful, or productive in the present moment, thus getting into the vibration which will attract what we desire. If we wait for life to be perfect before we take action, nothing will be achieved. The when/then attitude—for example, "When I get that promotion, then I'll be able to..."—can also be expressed as, "If only I had" or "I'll be happy when." Also, there needs to be less emphasis on doing, and much more on being. We need to do everything we can to feel that whatever it is we have chosen is already with us. This is called "behaving as if."

And so we recite affirmations, which are an effective tool for achieving goals and dreams, but we must express them as current, and positive. Affirmations are spoken aloud because sound vibrations are an excellent means of communication with the subconscious mind. For example: "I'm slim, attractive and popular," could be a suggestion for those who struggle with their appearance, rather than, "I will lose a stone and then people will find me attractive." However, obviously absurd statements such as, "I am a millionaire with an apartment in Monaco and a yacht in the marina," will be rejected by the subconscious because it recognises our lack of conviction as we make them. To address this, **Christy Marie Sheldon** suggests asking "lofty questions." For example, "I wonder why life is so good to me?" or "I wonder why the Universe keeps sending me so much money?"

Those who have studied personal development will have embraced these and related principles, and understand the value of a positive mental attitude. Our energy, vibrations and attitude to life also have an enormous influence on health, which will be discussed much further in Chapters 7, 8 and 9.

Choose Your Vibrations

The difference is very noticeable when you compare being in the presence of a long-term miserable person with encountering someone who is happy and fulfilled. The joyful person radiates positivity, and we even use words like "vibrant" to describe them. Consider Oprah, Tony Robbins or Richard Branson. These are examples of life's achievers.

Vibrant, of course, means not just vibrating but doing so very fast, at a high frequency. Every single thing is vibrating, even inanimate objects such as rocks, but clearly you would never describe a rock as vibrant.

We label people as energetic or lazy, and it's obvious which type has the higher vibration. Vibration, simply, is energy. Happy, healthy people have natural energy and are usually engaging in some sort of activity. Their emotions will be ranging from love, gratitude, confidence and enthusiasm, down as far as maybe hopefulness. By the time we descend to ambivalence, for example, the vibrations are already fairly slow.

The lowest vibration is fear. Down here, we feel like victims of circumstance and have no motivation to take steps to improve our situation, push back or stand up for ourselves. Religious and education systems leaders—and governments—are well aware of this and, where feasible, will use the media to progress their agendas. This is why it is strongly recommended to spend as little time as possible watching the news. Most of it is biased, and it isn't only in third world countries that television is used as a clever and insidious means of conditioning the population. Of course, we are all aware how advertising is the most blatant form of brainwashing, but at least it isn't presented as anything else.

Sometimes it can be difficult to differentiate between feelings and emotions, so what is the difference? Emotions are of the mind, but feelings are of the body. We even use the word "visceral" to describe feelings—this comes from the Latin word "viscera," which means the organs of the trunk: heart, liver and intestines.

There is a UK charity, established in 1994, called Look Good, Feel Better, which now operates internationally and was set up to help cancer victims regain their confidence after months of treatment which has frequently ravaged their appearance. Trained volunteer makeup professionals run classes using makeup donated by the big cosmetic brands. Patients experiment with the cosmetics, which they take home after the session, and they report dramatic improvements in spirits and consequently health. It's a clear example of how steps can be taken, by doing something practical, to raise vibrations.

Upscale your vibration when you are aiming for attraction and resonance. Actively raise your vibration using any means possible: Bring back happy memories (remembering how you *felt* at the time); watch uplifting videos, films and TV programmes; strenuously limit the time spent on miserable content - this includes the "News"; and choose happy, uplifting music. If you are feeling down, go for a run, take a walk in the sunshine, in nature if you can. If these options aren't practical in the moment, take a shower, dress up, and put on makeup (if appropriate for you!)

Life Is a Celebration

As I write, in early 2021, the UK is in lockdown again. Half the world is still enduring house arrest, confined to quarters, kept apart from extended family and loved ones. Plenty have been bereaved, in addition, and I for one am very cognisant of the suffering through which most populations are navigating.

I was on a Zoom call recently with a coach from an Australian outfit, who was frankly annoying in his glib dismissal of the huge tribulations and deep concerns about the future that I suggested were affecting large numbers of people. He just didn't get it! Because he lived in sunshine, clearly had a big house and garden, and had enjoyed his brief working-from-home experience (the Australian situation was contained very successfully), he was speaking from the planet called "I'm Alright Jack!"

Whilst I recognise how good this might be for his own vibrations, I still suggest that others might legitimately baulk at his self-satisfaction and complacency. In short, tact and diplomacy are still in fashion, and I think he would do well to consider his audience. Maybe I'm wrong? Should we really only consider ourselves? That just isn't the space from which many of us prefer to operate.

Rant over! These are very unusual times, and I suppose we are all learning to cope in our own way. Of course, it's good advice to find the positive in every situation—albeit sometimes it can be well hidden! And to say "everything happens for a reason" is not fatalistic. Because, if we can be objective—that is, attempt to view the situation as a dispassionate outsider—it can help us address any grief, disappointment or frustration. Yes, it could be a challenge to do so, more often than not! But, for example, several people including myself have, during lockdown, done things they would not otherwise have found time for. My garden looked pretty good last summer, and all that additional fresh air and exercise didn't do me any harm either!

My peers and I are involved in continual learning, personal development and, indeed, goal seeking. What we have learned to make a point of doing, is rewarding ourselves even for the little "wins." This is truly good for the subconscious, because it is actual training in the skill of expectation. It can become somewhat tedious always to be striving for completion, for the ultimate success, whilst in the meantime we just "keep on keeping on" (especially when one day is much the same as another!). So recognise the small successes—there are plenty of them—and when you set yourself the task of noticing them, you realise how much in your life is already good!

I'm in several mastermind groups and, frequently at meetings, participants have to start by reporting their wins. Sometimes no effort is required; but at other times, a person has to dig quite deep to remember anything of any consequence. Here's where the gratitude diary comes into its own. There are different ways of doing this—especially if you are busy—but as a minimum, write down three things daily for which you are grateful. It's hard to be despondent when you are pulling high-vibration thoughts to the fore.

Also, it's quite fun looking back over past entries and indeed past years of these gratitude journals. So keep your vibrations high, and treat yourself kindly! Remember the love, seek excuses—wherever and whenever—and just find a way to celebrate!

Attitude, vibration and celebration go hand in hand with health, and excellent health results from harmony in mind, body and spirit. The control we have, as individuals, over our internal environment, is far greater than most of us once imagined, and the next chapter will describe the importance of energy, and connection with spirit in our daily lives.

Chapter 7

Mind, Body and Spirit in Harmony

"One must marry one's feelings to one's beliefs and ideas. That is probably the only way to achieve a measure of harmony in one's life."
Napoleon Hill

Energy Medicine

Seventeen years ago, as the result of a freak accident, I sprained my back. Suddenly I found myself up close and personal with the limitations of modern medicine, especially as far as pain control was concerned. The so-called experts have no solutions for chronic pain, and sufferers feel that nobody cares, that no one is listening. At one time, I was reluctantly taking four different medications, prescribed by private specialists, whilst slowly moving up the waiting list to attend an NHS pain clinic. In desperation, I was forced to seek help elsewhere, and my boss recommended a local Spiritualist Church, which held monthly healing sessions. This was where I first encountered meditation, and "healers" who were able to address my pain, at least to an extent.

Regrettably, they were unable to solve the problem completely, and against my will, I had become a long-term consumer of pain medication. I was concerned about becoming addicted, quite apart from the fact that considerable pain was still clouding my life. Then, very fortunately, I crossed paths with a brilliant chiropractor who also practiced organ release. After just a few months of treatment, I was at last pain free! My interest in energy medicine, and all matters spiritual, has developed from this experience.

We all have the power to heal our own bodies. Everything, whether seen or unseen, is energy. Even what appears to be solid is merely compressed energy. Only comparatively recently has science caught up with this information and its game-changing relevance to life as we perceive it. A few people can see energy; for example, in the form of auras surrounding other people. Others recognised that they were able to access something external and utilise this for healing. It's the principle behind Reiki, a well-known form of energy healing. Acupuncture, acupressure and reflexology tap into the meridians or energy pathways in the body. The Chinese refer to *chi*, and tai chi is the now well-known practice of slow, controlled exercise, which harnesses energy and influences its flow within the body.

A few years ago, I took a course in Theta Healing, which regrettably didn't come naturally to me, although I found the concept fascinating and still have as yet unfulfilled intentions of taking further studies. Then, early in 2020, I came across **Dr Sue Morter's** book, *The Energy Codes*. Dr Sue is a chiropractor, as was her father, one of the pioneers in energy medicine. She was able to see auras, as a child, but soon realised that it wasn't exactly wise to discuss these with other people, as the reactions she received were off-putting to say the least. As she grew, she lost the skill. This is probably typical of the experiences of many children; they have perceptive skills in early life which are lost quite early due to lack of use, and lack of understanding by adults.

Humans, as tripartite beings, are composed of mind, body and spirit. Spirit can be replaced with "soul," and this can be represented by the breath, because when the breath leaves the body for the final time, this is the end of life.

Dr Sue emphasises the importance of the body, how it is constantly signalling to us, and how we miss its signals because we are "living in our heads." Her book brings together and makes sense of so much of the information that I had been accumulating since my accident, that I wasted no time in visiting her website and taking matters to the next level—and I am now certified to use the Energy Codes teachings in my coaching and training businesses.

The Energy Codes

This is the trademark name given by **Dr Sue Morter** to the principles and breathing practices that she developed, having had a profound and transformational experience during meditation. She spent several years working out how she could recapture the moment, even teach it to others, and so the procedures were born. Since reading her book, also entitled *The Energy Codes,* you could say that I have become one of her disciples, having undergone higher levels of training and qualified as a practitioner.

A deeper study of the philosophies behind the Energy Codes reveals just how we have attracted people and events into our lives, and the knowledge can be liberating. Dr Sue uses something she calls "The Bus Stop Conversation" to explain soul contracts and why unbelievably bad things might happen to some of us. This is discussed further in a later section of this chapter. When we embrace the concept that we make our own luck, the question naturally arises: How could some appalling circumstance actually be something of our own choosing? If a soul chooses this life to learn lessons or experience certain emotions, what happens as a result of that choice will manifest during the life of the soul. Of course, during this life, very few of us are actively aware of such contracts, because the process of being born is considered so intense and so disruptive that the mind and soul disconnect, and the only way that the soul can communicate with the mind thereafter is through the body. The mind has to be trained to pick up the signals that the body sends to the brain.

Most of us have come up against plans that never come to fruition, effort that appears to be wasted, and money that has been spent in vain. What's happening here? You may have heard the term "blockages" used by way of explanation when success or even progress towards goals remains stubbornly elusive. What are these blockages? Why are some people affected more than others? Can we do anything about them?

Let's consider the chakras, of which there are seven within the body, lined up along our spinal column. They are centres of energy, or light, vibrating at different frequencies, and so are depicted using the 7 colours of the rainbow, starting with red at the base and moving up to violet (or white) at the top of the head (the crown chakra). Each chakra governs specific abilities, such as wisdom, power, love, communication and even manifesting. Detail on the individual chakras follows in the next section, but ideally they are all connected by a central channel, in which we identify four "anchor points."

We encourage the chakras to rotate freely as we direct Earth energy and cosmic energy up and down the central channel, using breathing practices taught in the Energy Codes. When gaps exist in the pathway, these act as circuit breakers, and the energies cannot flow without interruption back up the column. These gaps are our blockages, and within the Energy Codes is the methodology for building circuits and joining up the gaps. Broadly speaking, these remedial practices involve a combination of breathing, mindfulness and focus.

With our blockages cleared, we can propel energy from Mother Earth with sufficient and uninterrupted force straight up this central column, and out of the body at the crown chakra (like water through a whale's blowhole). The energy will then shower down around us as it was designed to do, allowing us to fire on all cylinders.

All of us are surrounded by our personal energy fields, and it is these that connect us to each other via the Field, or Divine Matrix. Blockages result in weaknesses in the flow of Earth energy upwards along the column. So the showering effect is diminished and uneven, and we perceive life through a distorted field, delivering a distorted view of everything that happens to us.

The Chakras

It's important to have an understanding of the seven chakras, which are a string of vibrating power houses of energy situated along our spinal column. If these little vortices of energy are not fully operational, or unable to connect with each other because of gaps in the pathway, then it feels like we are stuck, being held back. We even use the phrase "self-sabotage." The higher chakras will not function properly when there are blockages lower down, and this is extremely common. For completeness, I will summarise the main characteristics of each chakra, together with what is experienced on different sides of the model of awakening (discussed later in the chapter), depending on whether or not the chakra is fully operational.

The *root chakra* is right at the base of the spine. It is coloured red and governs self-mastery, groundedness and health. To recognise where it is, squeeze mula bandha, the Sanskrit word for "root lock." (To locate this muscle, which lies at the base of the pelvic bowl, imagine that you were going to the bathroom and had to stop the stream suddenly.) When the root chakra is not operating at full strength, the results are mental lethargy, spaciness, incapacity for inner stillness, poor general health, specifically osteoarthritis, and also lack of vital energy. It is quite surprising how many people go through life completely disconnected from this chakra—being unaware of it, of course—and living with the consequences.

Working upwards, the next chakra is the *sacral chakra*, which governs the sex organs and the adrenals. This is the wisdom chakra, also governing trust, creativity and emotions. When operating out of kilter, it results in feelings of isolation, impotence, emotional instability and low back pain.

Chakra number three is the *solar chakra*, being located just below the diaphragm at the solar plexus. It is said to have the power of 1,000 suns (this is the literal translation of its Sanskrit name), and it governs personal power, respect of self and others, spontaneity and inhibition. It's the chakra of the pancreas, stomach and digestive organs and the autonomic nervous system.

The *heart chakra*, coloured green, is just behind its namesake organ and governs connection to all, compassion, unconditional love and the thymus gland. When this chakra is underperforming, we are subject to fear of betrayal, codependency, shallow breathing, high blood pressure, heart disease and cancer.

Chakra five, the *throat chakra,* is the manifesting chakra, but it cannot perform if the lower chakras are not fully operational and supplying it with energy. It governs communication, successful meditation, and artistic inspiration. Neck ache, asthma, perfectionism and inability to express emotions will result from issues with this chakra.

The sixth chakra is known as the *pineal gland*, or *third eye* because it contains rods and cones like the external eyes, although buried deep behind the centre of the forehead. It supplies insight, sometimes "second sight," perception of multiple dimensions, and ESP. Before activation, it can be responsible for nightmares, learning difficulties, hallucinations, headaches and poor vision.

Finally, the *crown chakra* is situated right at the outside of the crown, governing the central nervous system and also the pineal gland. When inactive, it can result in depression, obsessional thinking, chronic exhaustion and Alzheimer's disease. In full expression, as on the front side of the model, it provides personal magnetism and charisma, miraculous achievement, transcendence and collaboration with higher purpose.

The Model of Awakening

In *The Energy Codes*, **Dr Sue Morter** introduces the term "The Quantum Flip"—it's the sudden realisation that no matter what is happening to us, it's all good! We are the creators, the masters of our own ship. Our lives are happening for us, rather than to us. Regrettably, it does not feel like this for many of us, but understanding and applying the principles within the Energy Codes will lead to transformation and awakening.

To explain this in more detail, **Dr Sue** uses the following model: Imagine a coin, standing on edge with the two sides—heads and tails—in view. **Dr Sue** refers to the front side (where we live as our Soulful Selves) and the back side of the model (where our Protective Personalities rule). It's obvious which is going to be the preferable side!

As you visualise the model, you might be wondering about the descriptions "Soulful Self" and "Protective Personality," so I will briefly describe both: As the name suggests, the Soulful Self has the soul in charge, and so everything is wonderful, happening as intended; in fact, as the soul has decreed. This is full creatorship. All of us can aspire to it—residence on the front side—but the way I see it, living on the front side begins with a series of visits, which gradually grow in length. Because, life will continue to throw challenges at us, and so we might flip over to the other side quite often, but we will recognise what has happened and know what steps to take to get back to the front side.

So what is the Protective Personality, and why use this word "protective?" This takes us to the subject of the reptile brain, the most powerful and fastest reacting part of our subconscious. Its main purpose is to keep us safe. As we grow up and learn how to navigate life, this part of the brain learns from all our experiences of pain—physical and mental—and does a commendable job of preventing us from re-exposing ourselves to pain for which lessons have already been learned. This is how we pick up "limiting beliefs," also known as subconscious interference—and we have stored up a huge number of them by the time we are five years old! We continue to add to the store throughout our lives, and many get there just by listening to comments made by parents, teachers and people we love or respect.

A large number of limiting beliefs are connected with money: "The love of money is the root of all evil"; "It's easier for a camel to get through the eye of a needle, rather than for a rich man to get into heaven." Holding such beliefs keep us poor; and once recognised, we can address and dispel the power they have over us. But what about those beliefs that we haven't or can't identify? These generally involve fear, anger, love, sadness, enjoyment or judgement. The good news is that they can be cleared, even without our identifying them! B.E.S.T. Release, the Morter March and the mPower step, as taught by Dr Sue and her disciples, are powerful tools for clearing subconscious interference.

There are plenty of apparently successful, high powered business people who are still operating on the wrong side of the model, who might perceive the label "protective" as wholly inaccurate; so for this reason, we may substitute the term "Performance Personality."

It's also relevant to mention that I see the back side of the model as a spectrum. Right over at the far end of the range, the place that Dr Sue refers to as the back side of the back side, is pure victimhood. Most people are somewhere along the spectrum, closer to the coin, but may be suffering from what we would call the blame game: "He/she did this to me, so ...." Really close to the front side and the flip, we find ourselves making the best of things, making lemonade out of lemons, but still reacting to life rather than making it happen. Survivorship is the best description of life on the wrong side of the model.

Make the Quantum Flip, and you are living in creatorship. You recognise that you are in charge. You are the master of your own ship, designing your own life, and it's all good! Your life is full of serendipity, and the right people drift towards you just as you need them. So now you aspire to stay on that side for longer and longer periods.

The lengthier your stay on the front side, the better it gets. Your confidence is amazing; you are a brilliant communicator, open to all possibility. Life gets bigger and broader; your chakras are spinning at full strength and in full communication with each other. You are charismatic, at peace with everything, realising your higher purpose and closing in on, "I am all that there is!"

Luck and Manifesting

Some people just seem to have been born lucky; for others, life is apparently nothing but struggle and setbacks. As we begin to question the fairness, or otherwise of this observation, it's likely that our investigations lead us to the idea that we create our own luck.

So what is luck? Why do some of us seem to attract the wrong people and events into our lives? Most of us have come up against grand plans that never come to fruition, massive effort that appears to have been wasted or huge sums of money spent in vain. Even worse, really terrible events happen to a great many people, along the lines of child abuse, domestic violence, devastating car accidents caused by drunken drivers, and so on. Considering the statement that we make our own luck, how can those afflicted by such disasters have invited them into their lives?

As mentioned earlier, one of the deepest concepts discussed in *The Energy Codes* is "The Bus Stop Conversation," an allegorical explanation of soul contracts. Imagine a bunch of souls, awaiting their return to Earth for the next life, and a conversation starts up about why each is heading back, and what they hope to learn from their next life experience. This builds on the idea of soul purpose: that every soul selects about half a dozen lessons to learn from each sojourn here on Earth (or elsewhere, for that matter!)

Also, it is believed that groups of souls tend to make these journeys at the same time. Past life regression therapy has identified that patients recognise individuals from their present lives, popping up as different characters in past lives. See *Many Lives, Many Masters,* by **Dr Brian Weiss**. So, one soul might announce that they want a "level-10 experience in forgiveness," because right at the end of their previous life, they discovered forgiveness only shortly before death. It felt so good that they want the experience over again but in its fullest version—and they are looking for someone to help them achieve this goal.

Asked to expand on the sort of circumstance they envisage, the soul might go into dramatic and unpleasant detail about the sort of suffering and ordeals that they think will fulfil this requirement. Finding a volunteer to supply, for example, the drunken driver or the abusive relative, could require much persuasion... but the soul who agrees to fulfil the first soul's desire, is offering the most profound love, compassion and commitment. This is manifesting at the highest level.

To manifest just means to bring into being, and we all do this every single day. Yet we perceive the term similarly to casting some kind of spell, and strive to apply manifesting to the difficult ideas dreamed up by our thoughts and imagination. Frequently we fail to deliver, and question why this should be. The term "blockages" was discussed earlier, along with the use of specific breathing practices that can be applied to clear them. But sometimes we have diligently practiced all kinds of techniques that are calculated to deliver success as we pursue our goals, so how do we explain that occasionally we just can't reach the intended destination?

We have to accept that sometimes the timing is the one thing over which we have no control. It's essential to keep the faith, and eventually the thing will happen—assuming that it's meant to be, that is! The spiritual Universe does not recognise time, and it can happen that patience has to be employed—much patience—until suddenly we try again, find that all obstacles have disappeared, and the thing happens so easily that we wonder what on Earth was stopping us. Answer: It wasn't anything on Earth; it was Divine Right Timing.

Referring back to the model, manifesting is easy when we operate from creatorship, from the front side of the model. If we can access our highest vibrational energy, starting with building the circuits as recommended, a new paradigm is within our reach. Unbelievable power is within our grasp when we truly appreciate that life is supposed to happen through us rather than to us. Our power lies dormant until we recognise that its source is actually just another aspect of ourselves.

Into the Zone

Athletes at the top of their game are so focused on winning that they think of absolutely nothing else as they run the race, lift the weight or play the game. Watch an athlete as he or she prepares mentally, whilst awaiting the starter's gun. Pure concentration and laser focus, fully engaged, gives them a sort of fairy dust, enabling them to be better than their best, at exactly the time when it matters most.

Operating in the zone is particularly visible, for example, when we watch top tennis players. I'm not particularly sporty but have loved Wimbledon ever since moving to England. It's part of the summer, and tradition, and millions of us missed Wimbledon greatly last year when the organisers reluctantly accepted that they had no choice but to cancel. Every single sport was affected by the pandemic, of course, even the Tokyo Olympics, which will go ahead either later this year or not at all. Even if it happens, there will be no international spectators, a disappointment for millions.

Back to tennis, if you have watched the greats, such as Roger Federer, you will know what I mean when I say that at times a sort of magic seems to be in action as they play. Federer's performance has always looked remarkably effortless as he somehow positions himself in exactly the right place to return even the most impossible of balls fired at him by his opponent. "He'll never make it," you think, and then he seems to fly across the court, employing split-second timing and precision, as his racket connects with the opponent's missile.

Sometimes it looks like his return will be a miss hit, but against the odds he drops the ball just over the net, with so little bounce that there is no way the opponent can reach it in time. Then there are those incredibly strong backhand returns, when it seems that the ball just has to land well outside the court; and yet at the last minute, it curves back to land just fractionally on the right side of the line, thanks to exactly the right amount of spin somehow attached to it by the master. Yes, the brilliance displayed by tennis players operating in the zone is a sort of top-level autopilot, achieved by tapping into creatorship and engaging the utmost levels of skill, proficiency and expertise.

Stock market traders know that logic can be their worst enemy as they make split-second decisions that result in eye-watering losses or astronomical profits. Their decisions can be time sensitive, or dependent upon ever-fluctuating price levels. They have to act calmly and dispassionately, often within in a truly frenetic environment. **Mark Douglas** wrote *Trading in the Zone* as a handbook to assist with training and achieving this critical skill.

You may have noticed very skilled speakers using no notes or prompts, yet delivering fascinating and engaging discourses on subjects close to their hearts. Some even refer to this as channelling, the inference being that some higher power is conveying a message using them as the agent. Others are just so fired up by the ideas that they want to convey, that they become unstoppable, and their energy and enthusiasm are infectious.

Probably all of us have had the experience of engaging in something we love, often a hobby, and completely losing track of time. When we love our work, especially to the point where it no longer feels like work, we can find that we access this state, also known as the "flow state," quite regularly.

In their fascinating book *Stealing Fire*, **Steven Kotler** and **Jamie Wheal** discuss the related topics of group flow, altered states and "flipping the switch". They reflect upon how modern technology and scientific advances have led to amazing capabilities in terms of inducing states of superconsciousness, once possible only after years of training or hours of meditation. They explain the popularity of excessively risky "extreme sports", the power behind non-ordinary consciousness and describe all manner of advances in neuroscience and chemical engineering used to induce addictive peak experiences.

Unsurprisingly, all this knowledge about energy and how to use it, will not work in isolation. Awareness of all forms of pollution, of which there is a great deal in our modern lives, enables us to be selective in terms of what we breathe, ingest or touch. Equally important, though, is the attention we pay to our mental environment, which is not only subject to numerous subtle forms of pollution but also to sundry forms of stress that have dramatic effects on our health. The next two chapters discuss these factors, so please read on for a reminder of most of the areas over which we have influence, and of measures we can take to protect ourselves.

Chapter 8

Media, Money and Control

*"The secret to success is to own nothing,
but control everything."*
Nelson Rockefeller

Censorship

The indomitable Mary Whitehouse made quite a name for herself in the UK in the 1970s and 1980s, as leader of the NVALA (the National Viewers' and Listeners Association). She campaigned tirelessly about the content of television programmes of the era—and must be revolving in her grave in current times—for there were only three channels to monitor in the UK back then.

But Mrs Whitehouse wasn't only against love scenes and nudity, although indeed one of her major campaign areas was against the permissive society. For example, she tried to raise awareness of how TV coverage of the Brixton and Toxteth riots (1981) was glorifying the violence of an ongoing situation, actually encouraging others to join in the "fun." The police recognised the value of her warnings, and ordered that TV coverage of the riots be toned down.

She was active from the 1960s through to the 1990s; and rather sadly, her name is remembered as a comical King Canute-type character, trying to hold back the rising tide of "filth and pornography," as she described it. It's a fact that the majority of people who used to complain about censorship were aware of it only in the sense that they were being denied access to certain types of entertainment. Probably all were familiar with the censorship of the Film Board, and that television producers had to comply with comparable, very stringent regulations. Even in the days of black and white TV, at least one episode of *The Avengers* fell foul of these strict rules (I refer to the story about the Hellfire Club).

The rise of the internet has meant that anyone who wants to view materials of any kind, including pornography possibly beyond the imaginations of most of us, can acquire this, at little or no cost and merely at the press of a few buttons. Teenagers and even younger people may access hard-core porn at will, which invariably distorts their views of life and, critically, of relationships. Frequently, there is minimal cost to begin with; punters are drawn in and then have to pay incremental amounts as the "story" continues.

There used to be what was best called a gentleman's agreement between the royal family and the press. Famously, Edward VIII (later the Duke of Windsor) was pursuing an affair with a twice-divorced American, and this was discreetly and successfully withheld from the British public. When the news broke, he provoked a constitutional crisis by proposing to her, eventually choosing marriage over the Crown, which involved his agreement to abdication and acceptance of exile in France.

Of course, this could not happen now; such deference changed absolutely with Diana, Princess of Wales. She was an acknowledged master at manipulating the press, successfully making her own views and position known. This was used against her in the end, however, and the so-called paparazzi were made to shoulder much of the blame for her untimely demise in the Alma Tunnel in Paris, in 1997. Such is the pressure of being in the public eye, that her younger son Prince Harry and his wife recently chose to live abroad, distancing themselves from the family, stating that this was in preference to suffering relentless press scrutiny. They have built on the Diana model, as displayed in a recent, skilfully stage-managed interview with Oprah Winfrey.

There has been a rather more insidious form of censorship rife in society for 20 years or more, and that's the tyranny of political correctness. It started as a bit of a joke (comparable to the absurdity of some of the health and safety rules and warnings), but before long, people were being fired for making thoughtless remarks, even at private gatherings. A Northern MP famously lost her position after telling a questionable joke at a private dinner party, and being reported by one of the other guests. A panel TV presenter, while socialising after a particular show, made an unflattering remark about a tennis player, and the program host took such offence that he fired her from the panel of guest presenters. My point is, we have all had to become accustomed to guarding our speech, refraining from saying what we really mean and always being on the alert against giving offence. What has happened to free speech? To quote **Charles**

Bradlaugh, "Better a thousandfold abuse of free speech than denial of free speech."

Social Media

In January 2011, I recall listening to nightly radio reports as the Arab Spring riots progressed. I wondered vaguely why they blamed social media for assisting these large gatherings to happen. At the time, I had little or no knowledge of Facebook, which then had vastly less power than it has today. Now that I understand more, I appreciate that activists were presumably members of local groups—a great way of spreading information to a selected band of relevant people.

Wind forward a few years, and although I resented the intrusive nature of the sign-up procedure, I nevertheless joined Facebook on a "can't beat 'em, join 'em" basis. Everybody I knew in business was on Facebook, and every training establishment that I joined had a group. I was supposed to promote myself and my business on there, and post with enthusiasm. It didn't take long before I realised that most of the people I knew were presenting entirely false personas, as they puffed themselves up claiming all sorts of successes that I knew they didn't really have. *Visibility is credibility* has become the general mantra.

This is another example of perception and manipulation: People validate ideas (no matter how accurate or otherwise) by "liking" posts on Facebook, Twitter and the rest. The more "likes" one collects, the more truthful one's offering is perceived to be in the minds of others! With YouTube, validity is measured by the number of views.

The young of today appear to have embraced all the numerous platforms available, with confidence, enthusiasm and utter disregard of privacy! I suspect many would declare that privacy is an outdated concept; that is, supposing they even understand the word. Yet it should be noted that not only the young were tripped up when the *Cambridge Analytica* scandal broke in 2018. These researchers had used an app (developed in 2014!) to harvest personal details relating to millions of Facebook users, without requesting permission. The data was used to target voters in various election campaigns, including Donald Trump's and possibly Brexit, hence the publicity and uproar. Nobody noticed anything was amiss until politics became involved.

This has been seen as a wake-up call for users of social media—you will recall the publicity—but I see it as no more than a natural consequence of so much data being requested, held and freely given to a giant such as Facebook. Why did this abuse of privacy come as such a shock?

So, now that we have all been suitably chastened about sharing too much information, what about the wrong sort of images? On all platforms—Instagram, Tumblr, Pinterest, TicTok—new ones are appearing all the time, and I struggle even to keep up with the originals! Once an image is "out there" in the ether, you can never reclaim it, even if you delete the offending post. LinkedIn seems to have much to offer business people; connect with me on that one if you are interested: http://tiny.cc/linkac.

Confession time: I do not use social media enough. I recognise its value as a business tool, and within business circles, Facebook could be invaluable. But posting has never been uppermost in my mind. Many of my peers (the female ones!) actually worry about what they are wearing on holiday, because of how it will look when they post! All my posts have been business related, except possibly when I've been tagged by others. All well and good, I thought—and then I was told that should someone look me up, then they would want to see huge quantities of personal trivia as well. I had just begun to work on this, when Facebook kicked me off the platform!

I will never know why, but it had something to do with advertising: I was accused of "transgressing community guidelines"—make sense of that one! My major issue is that I absolutely could not connect with anyone on Facebook to discuss my case. So 28 days passed, and then I lost about nine years' worth of photos, posts, and more importantly, connections. I have set up a new profile, but truly I have minimal interest in playing their games, nor in ever attempting again to advertise and pay them money. However, I invite you to join my recently formed Crossover Coach Group at the following URL: http://tiny.cc/crossovercoach.

Strangely, as this Facebook situation was happening to me, **Donald Trump** was unceremoniously kicked off Twitter! How can it be that the President of the USA (who was probably their most prolific tweeter) is treated so shabbily? Apparently Facebook has banned him for two years. There is never any discussion. One day you are in, the next you are out. They will use you while it suits them, while you help with their reach, but your importance to them is less than zero. Very fortunately, I had always resisted the temptation to log into various other websites via Facebook, so I have lost nothing in that direction. I mentioned in Chapter 5 how the relentless alerts to trivia on social media are impacting concentration and production levels for the unwary—

we are all well advised to *switch off these alerts!*

YouTube might have been the first to join in the censorship argument—they have always felt free to delete content that they considered inappropriate—but matters got totally out of hand as the pandemic developed in 2020. Authors were being "de-platformed"—right, left and centre—and there were certain subjects which were simply not allowed. One of these was 5G radiation. We got to the ludicrous position where serious presenters were talking about it like this: "You know what I mean; the number that comes between 4 and 6, followed by the letter that rhymes with tea."

In Chapter 3, I spoke about fake news. How do you program an algorithm to recognise this? It simply is not possible. So all they can do is identify certain topics about which Control feels that discussion is dangerous! If you have time on your hands, and fancy a bit of a laugh, look up Flat Earth Society on YouTube. I think that this just has to be a tongue-in-cheek cover up for an anti-Illuminati set up.

Airbrushed from History

Nikola Tesla was at one stage known as the most intelligent man on the planet, even more so than **Albert Einstein.** Originally from Serbia, he emigrated to America in 1884. He was a hugely respected, talented scientist, and many of his patents still astonish some of today's top scientists. Yet I, as a science graduate, first heard of him only five or six years ago, and I suspect that the only reason his identity is now well known, is that **Elon Musk** decided to name his phenomenal electronic car after **Tesla**. Generations have been taught that **Einstein** was the leading light in physics, that **Edison** invented electricity, and that **Marconi** invented radio waves. That **Tesla,** the brains behind these and countless inventions credited to other people, was systematically edited out of textbooks and history until recently, is another example of the power of extreme wealth.

Unfortunately for **Tesla,** and indeed for the general public then and to this day, he fell foul of some of the richest men in the world. The scandal began when they commissioned him to create a self-driven, free energy generator using the energy that occurs in our environment, and he successfully achieved this. But rather than revealing plans for his free energy generator to the industrialists, **Tesla** naively presented them with the actual device.

The tycoons, who have never been named, were impressed and incredulous certainly, but realised that this marvellous invention would bankrupt all of them. Overnight, **Tesla** went from being a highly sponsored, ground-breaking scientist to being considered the greatest financial threat ever perceived by the wealthiest of the wealthy of that time. They saw to it that his plans for the generator were suppressed, his free energy projects were stopped in their tracks and all his funding was abruptly cut off. From this time onwards, he found it increasingly difficult to find investors for any of his projects.

Tesla opened the doors to communicating with extra-terrestrial frequencies that responded intelligently, and also claimed to know which frequencies could cure certain diseases. That much of his work in magnetism and electricity was later attributed to **Thomas Edison**, is down to the fact that **Edison** was an extremely astute businessman. At one time, he had employed Tesla. They fell out over money—Edison foreclosed on a loan—which caused extreme difficulty for the Serb. Towards the end of his long life, Tesla might have been suffering from OCD (not recognised at the time) and had become increasingly solitary. He lived a very healthy lifestyle, was largely vegetarian and gave a fascinating interview in 1935 about the relevance of exercise and lifestyle on overall health.

At the time of his death, in 1943, **Tesla** had for years been living alone in the New Yorker Hotel and was more or less penniless. There were rumours that he was working on a "death ray" machine, which supposedly was a weapon to end all wars, and on flying saucer propulsion systems. Aged 86, he died surrounded by his papers, which were swiftly seized by the FBI, on the grounds that they must be kept away from enemy hands. This meant, specifically, the Soviet Union. **J Edgar Hoover**, head of the FBI at the time, sent **John Trump** (uncle of former President **Donald Trump**) to inspect and assess the papers, deciding on whether they were relevant to national security or not.

It was announced that they contained nothing of importance, but according to **Margaret Cheney**, author of *Tesla: Man Out of Time*, many of the documents, inventions and patent applications were simply never released into the public arena. If Cheney is correct, then **John Trump** did find items of importance there, which for whatever reason, have never surfaced. It seems that there is revived interest today in the free energy generator plans, and there are plenty of stories on the net about DIY enthusiasts who, having somehow obtained secret files, are now generating free electricity for themselves.

Compliance and Manipulation

Liberty is not an absolute value. It can be overwritten in extreme cases, so we might wonder whether the current (COVID-19) circumstances have been sufficiently extreme for this to have happened. A disease with a 99% recovery rate does not appear to justify the confinement and isolation of healthy people, which we have been suffering for the major part of the past year. **Lord Sumption,** a retired Supreme Court Justice, is one of the many who have voiced doubts about the lockdown policy and the Civil Contingencies Act (see Chapter 5). He maintains that risk is an inherent part of human existence, and asks what degree of risk should be acceptable.

This is a value judgement, as is what steps should be taken to avoid the risk and what the alternatives are. In the lockdown decision, it appears that no value has been attached by governments worldwide to economic devastation, educational disruption and damage, nor to the deprivation of interaction with other humans. Touch is a basic human need, and there is more to life than avoidance of death. People were deprived of contact with dying relatives and denied attendance at their funerals. Those in the early stages of cancer were left without treatment. Battered wives and children were confined in dangerous spaces. Countless thriving businesses, of all sizes, failed as a result of forced closure. Loneliness and isolation, already more of an issue in our society than is acceptable, rose to shocking levels.

People who are sufficiently frightened and craving security will submit to almost anything. There is also a reluctance to speak out; whilst some share the fear, many are concerned about breaking ranks, and so give the appearance of sharing the prevailing view. Last month, I heard from a business connection of a group of solicitors within the UK, who wanted to challenge the enforced closure of public houses on viable legal grounds. Significant pressure was applied along the lines that if they went ahead with the case, they would never practise again.

There is coercion now that everybody should accept the COVID-19 vaccination, something which should be a matter of choice. It seems to have been become a badge of honour—people boast about having had the jab, and gloat as they warn those expressing reluctance that they will be denying themselves access to airline travel—and what's more, to regularly used facilities like pubs, restaurants, theatres and museums. In his comprehensive books, **David Icke** refers to Problem-Reaction-Solution. He is one of the many who has been de-platformed from YouTube, but he and numerous controversial speakers can be found on LondonReal.tv, which was set up by **David Rose** in response to the levels of censorship on YouTube. **Icke** has remarked that when people are acting as sheep, they actually police themselves—there is no need for sheepdogs in human society.

You might not have wondered whether a cause for the current economic meltdown will ever be admitted, or even identified. **Jim Rohn** tells us: *"If you don't design your own life plan, chances are you'll fall into someone else's plan. And guess what they have planned for you? Not much."* If you value independence and self-reliance, and can embrace ideas such as contrarianism or swimming against the tide, you will no doubt be aware that there is now a vast number of people claiming benefits who have never before had to do so.

We have to wonder why the decision was taken to crash the economy, whilst offering no financial help to the self-employed, nor to owner/directors of small companies in the UK. Dependency does not come naturally to a majority of our population, yet many have been left with nowhere to turn except benefits and foodbanks. This mystifying policy was adopted more or less simultaneously by all major governments. If conspiracy theories interest you, look up *Plandemic*, or visit LondonReal.tv as a starting point. If you have a little time to spare, these will open up a veritable rabbit warren for you to explore.

Organic Farming and Food Affordability

Back in mediaeval times, the population practised crop rotation, and for 1 year in 3, or sometimes 4, a field would be allowed to lie fallow; that is, no crop was grown and it was used for grazing, which added natural fertiliser to the land. So, the soil could recover, and the following year they would then plant cereals, which had the highest nutrient requirement from the soil. In years two and three, the crops would be peas, lentils or beans, which drew less because of nodes in their root systems. Such practices have long been abandoned in modern agricultural structures, all in the interests of making profit. Empty fields cost money—something must be produced! Pesticides are used in abundance to kill off weeds and insects, and when the soil is left with no natural fertility, just throw on a few tons of chemical fertilizer (followed by even more herbicide to stop the weeds going mad) and the problem is solved.

But is it? What effects are all these chemicals having on the bodies of the end consumers? **Rachel Carson's** famous book, *Silent Spring,* alerted the public and the authorities to the dangers in many chemicals, and led directly to the banning of DDT as a pesticide. So nowadays, controls on application of chemicals are very strict, but their use is still considered excessive by many. Pesticides kill off useful insects too, including the dung beetle, which is critical for spreading organic nutrients throughout the soil.

Hence the rise in interest in organic produce—food grown without any form of chemical intervention. Such foods are vastly more expensive, not due to profiteering but because so much more work is involved in production. Even today, organic farmers see themselves as pioneers, due to the lack of instruction manuals and the amount of time and energy that can be required to raise crops and animals organically. Volumes produced are necessarily lower—herds have pastures in which to roam, and hens are not confined indoors in cages, thousands to a shed. Even their feed is expensive, as it too must be organic. (The BSE scare in the UK in the 1990s was caused by the despicable practice of grinding up animal carcasses to provide commercial feed for the unfortunate stock animals kept by farmers. Not only would such animals be herbivores in nature, but contamination resulting from the use of carcasses, *even of diseased animals,* was identified as the cause of this devastating illness.)

So despite its increase in popularity, organic food remains a choice only for the better off, and out of reach of the poor. Even fresh produce is inaccurately perceived by many as something they can't afford, although I am aware of many television programmes attempting to bridge this gap. The disparity is noticeable particularly in the availability of snacks and fast food. Think of any garage or motorway service area where you might want to purchase a quick and convenient bite to take out and consume in the car. The price of a single apple or banana can exceed the price of a chocolate bar! A packet of crisps or other salty, greasy snack falls into the same price bracket. Because of the addictive properties of sugar, the chocolate bar will probably be selected. (Even I refuse to pay silly prices for fruit—I bring my own healthy snacks with me when I travel.)

Cereal bars are promoted as healthy, which is not necessarily true—just check out the sugar content! So apart from a sandwich, what's left as a simple, portable snack? Pasties, sausage rolls, filled croissants and similar? Plenty of high-calorie dross, with little nutrition. Some outlets offer little packaged salads, but the prices are high, and they are not exactly practical if you are driving.

Knowing all this in advance allows us to plan. Maybe a 10-minute rest stop, while we consume something with a fork or spoon. Beware of yoghurt—there is little good to say about it, although it has been cleverly marketed for years. Essentially, it is rotting milk with the nasty taste covered up by sugar and a little fruit; or worse still by synthetic sweeteners, colours and flavourings. Consider soup! Again, advance preparation might be needed, along with a Thermos flask—remember those? "Other brands are available"—and they are back in fashion for health-conscious consumers!

Factory Farming and Frankenstein Foods

Read up on factory farming and you will never want to consume anything but organic. Visit an abattoir and you might forever be turned away from eating dead flesh. Digest the fact that 20% of the American dairy herd is infected with antibiotic-resistant mastitis, and your sympathy might well up for the unfortunate cows suffering this painful condition, who are nevertheless milked daily. Learn that the USDA actually allows a certain percentage of pus contamination in the milk supplied to retailers and wholesalers, and you just might fall out of love with ice cream, cheese and cream, as well as with milk.

Incidentally, milk is not good for us. Nature designed it for baby cows, and for them it is perfect, but humans are actually supposed to be lactose (milk sugar) intolerant. That a majority of us can happily consume milk, strangely, is due to a genetic mutation! As mentioned in Chapter 3, various milk marketing boards successfully persuaded their country's education system to let them influence children as to the value of milk in the diet, and governments even distributed free milk in schools. Generations have grown up being taught to believe a giant lie, and we tend to remember the concepts we learn in our early years at school.

Suppose you have decided to forego meat, fish and animal produce (i.e. dairy). Is turning vegetarian a safe option? Regrettably, even here there is a minefield to navigate in the form of GMO, genetically modified organisms. I recall learning in the 1980s about what seemed then to be a brilliant innovation; a type of grain had been developed with twice the protein content of natural varieties, and which appeared to offer a cost-effective solution to feeding not only the poor but also acting as a sort of super grain in animal feed. However, early enthusiasm for developments dwindled as science "advanced" and GMO became widespread with its profit potential becoming fully appreciated by the food industry. Proliferation accelerated in the 1990s, and it was only in 2003 that the WHO and the FAO (United Nations) developed international standards for safety.

Find articles presenting GMO with a positive spin, and you will read that we have been successfully breeding hybrids for hundreds of years and that GMO isn't really much different— it's just that knowledge of science is now so great that we have much greater capability.

Read a few commentaries by disaffected scientists and you will appreciate why the safety debate has intensified. Honest scientists will admit that they do not truly know/understand the risks themselves, and that the regulators who rubber-stamp applications carry out no safety testing whatsoever. In truth, they wouldn't know where to start.

The facts are frightening. For example, GMOs including maize and soybeans are bred to contain a transgene that causes them to make their own inbuilt insecticide. If you don't like the thought of that, it gets worse: A single plant will contain many of these so-called "insect specific toxins," using a process known as stacking. Some of the toxins involved are disturbingly similar to the anthrax bacteria, or share structural similarities with the ricin molecule.

Many GMO crops are herbicide resistant, a fact which is allowing farmers to spray excessive quantities of weed killer on their crops, with the preferred chemical being the notorious glyphosate (Roundup) manufactured by Monsanto. That's probably enough scientific detail for this chapter—sufficient evidence that GMO foods should be avoided where at all possible. An additional problem is that not all countries insist on the labelling of GMO content in processed foods—so consumer choice is removed —and where the GMO grains are used in animal feed, the implications for the consumer are obvious.

Agribusiness is fast becoming as scary as Big Pharma—it just isn't talked about as much. Money and the inexorable quest for profit at all costs is flourishing, at the expense of the farmer, the consumer and the environment. As it becomes increasingly difficult to maintain a normal standard of health, this is showing up particularly in the raised obesity levels in mature economies. But there are steps we can take to optimise our chances, which I discuss in the next chapter.

Chapter 9

Mens Sana in Corpore Sano

"Science may have found a cure for most evils;
but it has found no remedy for the worst of them all—
the apathy of human beings."
Helen Keller

Are You Getting Enough?

One of the most effective methods of torture is sleep deprivation. Forcibly keep the prisoner awake, by means of bright lights, loud noise or forcing him to stay alert in order to maintain safety, and within a few days, he becomes completely disorientated and willing to deliver up whatever is being demanded. This was one of the methods used to identify witches in 16th-century Scotland—after 5 days or so, the poor women would be massively confused and panicky, suffering hallucinations, and in this state could be induced to admit to practically anything.

We all know that the body needs food, water and air to survive. But it also cannot operate without sleep. Numerous systems will not function normally; communication with the brain drops right off, and so quality of life can be dramatically lowered. When we are ill, sleep is often the best remedy. Minimal medication, combined with plenty of hydration and sleep, will improve and even cure a huge number of common ailments. As **Shakespeare** reminds us in *Macbeth*: "Sleep, that knits up the ravelled sleeve of care... chief nourisher in life's feast."

Lack of sleep causes memory issues and leads to trouble with reasoning and concentration, so work is affected. Mood changes occur, such as anxiety, depression or just bad temper. Being drowsy can lead to accidents. The immune system is weakened, because antibodies and cytokines are produced during sleep. Without these, resistance to common bugs such as colds and flu is diminished. Lack of sleep also leads to an increase in blood sugar levels, raising the risk of type 2 diabetes. Weight gain will occur because leptin, the chemical that signals "that's enough, I'm full," is no longer produced. Instead, grehlin levels are raised, which stimulate appetite. Some people wake up mid-sleep and crave food. Sleep deprivation can cause balance issues, risk of heart disease, low sex drive and high blood pressure.

Strangely, we feel we need to apologise for needing our full quota of sleep! Seven to seven and a half hours, on a regular basis, are recommended by experts. Many of us are operating well below this level and experience frequent yawning, irritability and daytime fatigue. We address this with stimulants such as coffee and carbonated energy drinks. Chocolate and tea also contain caffeine, producing that short-lived lift in our spirits. But although the immediate boost that we cherish so much might seem to wear off, this doesn't mean that the caffeine will have left our system by the time we go to bed. Sometimes we cannot get off to sleep; frequently we wake after a few hours and find that sleep eludes us for the rest of the night. Quite soon we can find ourselves in a cycle from which it's very difficult to break loose.

Margaret Thatcher famously required only four hours' sleep, and it became part of her fearsome reputation. However, details published by the National Archives in 2018, suggest that she might have made up for it (to an extent) by napping in her chauffeur-driven car. Power naps have become hugely popular in recent years, but they are far from a new-age fad. While the term "power nap" is a relatively new addition to our vocabulary, short afternoon naps have been around for centuries. **Winston Churchill, Napoleon** and **Thomas Edison** were documented nappers.

Disease and the Environment

Louis Pasteur is famous for creating the process of pasteurisation, and for inventing the first vaccination. He laid the foundation for eradicating smallpox, which was formerly a much-feared killer disease, with the small percentage who survived it being left with ugly pockmarked skin. He also carried out detailed investigations into an epidemic affecting silkworms. Moths with globules were indeed ill with one disease, but actually there were two diseases killing the silkworms. The globules were one type of microbe, and **Pasteur** identified a second disease that was previously unsuspected.

He further determined that environmental conditions such as temperature, humidity and sanitation affected susceptibility to both diseases, but **Pasteur** focused on the microbes themselves and developed what we call "germ theory." He laid the foundations for the ways illness and infection are still discussed today: that germs enter a healthy host and attack it, causing disease. Although smallpox was caused by a virus, Pasteur was working in the nineteenth century, before viruses had been isolated. The virus, already known to be tiny and particulate rather than liquid, was identified by **Thomas Milton Rivers** in 1926, who called it an "obligate parasite." The electron microscope, invented in 1931, eventually allowed scientists to see a virus for the first time.

Pasteur was originally a chemist, working in the very early days of investigation of how organisms succumbed to illness. He was a great orator, developing the work and theories of earlier scientists. He was even accused of plagiarism, and there was much opposition to his hypotheses. **Antoine Béchamp,** already a respected biologist, was one of his greatest rivals and believed instead that living entities created bacteria in response to host and environmental factors. In other words, disease stemmed from an unhealthy bodily system which triggered changes in minute particles of the body, leading to disease. This was called "host theory."

Béchamp theorised that germs were actually chemical by-products that arose when the body was in an unbalanced state. For disease to take hold, there already had to be some sort of cellular dysfunction, or a kind of decay causing dead tissue at different sites in the body. Then the opportunistic germs would show up and be able to take hold in a body that was already out of balance. Malnutrition, exposure to toxins, or insanitary conditions would cause the required imbalance.

So germ theory and host theory, at that time, were two radically different views of how people became ill, or acquired disease. **Pasteur** said that healthy people unfortunately "caught" colds and infections, whilst **Béchamp** maintained that it was the underlying health of the patient that caused him to succumb to illness. Because Pasteur was so convincing as a debater, and frankly a much better salesman, his theory won people over, and indeed became the standard theory still in use by the modern Western medical community.

Alexander Fleming discovered penicillin by accident, in 1928; since then, the use of antibiotic drugs has mushroomed to absurd proportions, so much so that many diseases have become antibiotic resistant. What was once seen as a quick fix, reducing recovery times dramatically, has largely lost its magic. Antibiotics were successful against most bacteria but did not work on viruses; hence, the declaration that there is "no cure for the common cold," nor in fact for almost anything caused by a virus.

The biggest problem is that germ theory does not work when we attempt to treat chronic diseases with drugs, because the drugs treat the symptoms and not the cause. What's more, many of the drugs are themselves poisoning the patients, causing side effects for which still more drugs are needed. Regrettably, few medics (nor their patients, of course) look at the influence of diet on disease. As a population, our tendency is to reach for highly processed convenience foods, cheap foods—often indistinguishable from junk foods—and sweet fixes in both solid and liquid form.

Other huge health problems in our modern world include cancers and autoimmune diseases such as multiple sclerosis, lupus, rheumatoid arthritis and inflammatory bowel disease. These diseases simply were not known until perhaps a hundred years ago. It is likely that our grandparents were not afflicted because their lifestyles were so much healthier, involving exercise, eating unadulterated, healthy foods, and they used natural remedies such as balms and herbal tinctures rather than drugs.

Nutrition and Natural Healing

At university, I read nutrition and biochemistry—quite ahead of my time, but I was interested in the subject matter—and very recently, "functional nutrition" seems to have become quite a hot topic! I have a doctor friend who has just "discovered" nutrition—unbelievably, the average doctor spends maybe half a day during their notorious 7 years of training, reviewing the importance of what we put into our bodies! Doctors' training centres on diagnosis and prescribing chemical remedies—a pill for every ill. Many of our chronic diseases, and the majority of cancers, can be improved if not eradicated by upscaling our diets, cutting out poisons such as sugar and drastically reducing animal protein. *The China Study* by **Colin Campbell**, which has been filmed as *Forks Over Knives,* sets out very clearly the arguments for limiting consumption of animal protein.

Type II diabetes (which used to be called adult-onset diabetes) has greatly increased in the West over the past 25 years—particularly in the USA and the UK—and the population will not be aware of having greatly changed its eating patterns. The hidden problem quite simply is excessive sugar consumption. I speak not only of refined sugar but of sugar substitutes—of which there are more than 50—with names like maltose, sucralose (beware anything ending in "ose"), not to mention that infamous culprit: corn syrup.

Adding corn syrup to soft drinks was one enormous confidence trick. It was massively cheaper for manufacturers to use, because smaller quantities are required for the same effect. However, the drinks got sweeter too, and most consumers didn't notice. That is to say, the products kept on selling! But corn syrup is enormously addictive, even more so than sugar.

Then there's the sugar which is hidden in the food we buy—it's in almost everything, even bread. If you have ever made jam, you will know how sugar literally melts into what you are making, huge quantities producing quite a small volume of result. Sugar has been used as a preservative for hundreds of years, but it isn't only used for this purpose today. There has been a proliferation of ready-to-cook foods developed, which are very popular in view of our busy lifestyles. Look through the ingredients on a packaged product that you perceive as "savoury," such as pasta in sauce, and you will be amazed how soon sugar appears in the list (constituents are presented in order of percentage content in the product).

Another con delivered to us by the insurance/diet/processed food Industries is that fat is bad for our health, and that we need low-fat diets in order to reduce weight. *Never* buy low-fat versions of anything! Not only is the logic flawed, but the fat was what produced the flavour. The missing fat is replaced with sugar—without it, fat-reduced food tastes like cardboard.

There's also the supersize con. Purchase a soft drink in a (already excessively big) container and the clerk will ask you if you want to "supersize" it for a small, extra fee. You think you're getting a great deal (although you do not need the extra volume); and for the seller, the deal is even better, probably more than 90% profit!

If we would just sort out our diets, removing as much processed food as possible, with particular reference to cutting out refined sugar, there will be noticeable and virtually immediate benefits: better skin, healthier hair, increased vitality, reduced brain fog and, of course, weight reduction.

A diet containing as much fresh fruit and vegetables as we can afford, will prevent what are described as "lifestyle diseases." For example, diabetes and age-related problems such as hypertension and Alzheimer's will disappear. Patients have healed themselves from cancers and autoimmune diseases by means of intention, mindset and healthy diet.

Louis Pasteur, mentioned earlier, was the inventor of the first vaccination, which protected against the frequently deadly scourge of smallpox, rampant at the time. But towards the end of his life, Pasteur himself said that "the terrain is everything; it isn't so much the pathogen." Pasteur had come around to **Béchamp's** way of thinking and was referring to the general health of the body, and to the environment. That is, the levels of cleanliness or otherwise, in which the illnesses lurk, ready to invade. Many doctors today readily acknowledge that it's largely insanitary conditions that cause outbreaks of disease, and that the near eradication of many illnesses, such as polio, is as much down to improved living conditions as it is to vaccination campaigns.

The Three-Brain Guidance System

All of us are well acquainted with the brain in our head. We call it our mind, our intellect or even our thought processer. We are trained to use it from infancy, and from our earliest years the educational system tends to cause us to favour either its left or right side, often at the expense of developing in a fuller more rounded manner. Our early development also trains us to "live in our heads"; in other words, to use our minds at every possible opportunity. Our busy brains are continually thinking, analysing and writing stories to make sense of everything that happens to us.

Working with the *Energy Codes,* we continually use the expression "take it to the body": When we are triggered, or experience a charge—if someone upsets us or we respond to an event—we need to ask the question, "Where in the body do I feel it?" Is it, for example, a tightness in the throat, an ache at the back of the neck, butterflies in the stomach or maybe a pain behind the eyes? Next time it happens, don't ask yourself, "What should I do about it?" but rather, "Where do I feel it?"

We think far too much. We waste hours analysing, planning, regretting, reliving and worrying. Most is unnecessary and unproductive—in short, it is a waste of time. We should rather develop the habit of switching off, or stilling the mind. Mindfulness, meditation and yoga are well-known calming practices, assuming you have a little time to set aside, along with a peaceful environment. There is also a quick and useful grounding technique, with which anyone can discharge! Just squeeze mula bandha, as described in Chapter 7, for a short while. Take a few belly breaths. This allows you quickly to get in touch with the root chakra. Keep the squeeze going for a minute or so, and your anger or frustration will have magically diminished.

How often have you just had a hunch, a feeling you couldn't exactly explain, that you ought or ought not to do something? Most of us recall occasions where we ignored that feeling and wished later on that we had in preference followed its advice.

It's remarkably rare for people who act on a hunch to regret doing so. It is more frequently reported that because of taking a certain action, such as catching a later train, or even cancelling a flight, that some positive result transpired. These are only the incidents that we notice and recall—it happens more than we realise. Another name for a hunch is a gut feeling—there really are receptors in the gut, in receipt of billions of messages or bits of information every second. Most of it, we filter out, but a small amount gets through and, subconsciously, we act on it. For example, we aren't aware of instructing our bodies to sweat or shiver when the temperature rises or falls, to breathe faster when we exercise, or to hit the brake when we perceive danger whilst driving. Yet most of us imagine that the gut is responsible only for digestion, while all actions, conscious and unconscious, are dealt with in the brain. But this is far from the case. The body is a holistic, vital system, and when the higher self, or spirit, wants to connect with the mind, it will talk to the body, often using the gut, but it also speaks to the heart.

Society has told us that logic is preferable to love. That old saying, "Don't let your heart rule your head," has done many of us no favours at all. Ancient cultures viewed the heart as a source of inner guidance for morality and decision making. The

Heart Math Institute has carried out numerous studies and has confirmed that the heart has its own independent nervous system and is worthy of the label "heart-brain." The heart emits a measurable electromagnetic force all around the body, extending out several feet. Clearly, the forces overlap when people are in close proximity: another way in which we are all connected.

The heart is designed to receive messages from the environment and send them up to the brain for interpretation and action. How much information do we miss because we forget that it's more than a muscle pumping blood around the body? In the brain, some messages reach the amygdala, the emotional processing centre. Hormones such as oxytocin (the cuddle hormone) are produced in response to love. Other messages reach the thalamus, which sorts and controls information passed up to the higher brain centres, those responsible for clarity of thought and decision making. A heart in a healthy state of coherence has the mind, brain and emotions in sync with each other, thus expanding the mind's ability to access intuition, to focus, have clarity of thought and see beyond our limitations.

Life in the Twenty-First Century

Stress is the body's way of responding to any kind of demand or threat. It is automatic, and part of the way that our reptile brain keeps us safe. The "fight or flight" mechanism releases adrenalin and cortisol into our systems, making the heart pump faster, shutting down digestion, and increasing blood supply to our muscles, thus enabling us to run with maximum speed and escape the sabre-toothed tiger or modern equivalent. The problem is that modern life can throw all kinds of low-level stress in our direction on a daily basis, and we never use the muscles or the massive potential spurt of energy which was intended to burn up the hormones and discharge the tension. And so cortisol remains in our systems, causing symptoms such as depression, autoimmune diseases, skin conditions and even weight gain. What many do not realise is that stress also depresses the body's immune system.

Almost all of us are affected by stress to an extent, and managing stress is an essential life skill. Despite all the technical and mechanical aids available to us, we are almost all under some kind of continual pressure, whether it's too much to do in too little time, overwhelm, balancing scarce finances, exhaustion, loneliness, fear about the future, or having insufficient or low-quality, nutrient-deficient food. Many suffer from what can be described as a generalised anxiety, for which they cannot identify a reason, but they find themselves unable to relax, sleep or concentrate. We need to recognise the different ways that stress can manifest, and learn to seek out and deal with the causes.

Stress is not always a bad thing: In short bursts, it can help with concentration and performance, increase strength for short periods and speed up reaction times. If we recognise when the "danger" has passed, and take steps to discharge, then all will settle down. The problem with ongoing or chronic stress is that it can creep up on us, and we get used to the feeling. It becomes normal and familiar. Common external causes include major life changes, ongoing issues at school or work, relationship difficulties or family and child-related challenges.

The situation arising from the COVID-19 pandemic has caused all kinds of additional physical stresses, ranging from loss of freedom, to lack of structure regarding education, and unfamiliar balancing of working from home with family management. Not to mention the internal stresses involved with worries about paying bills and what the work situation will provide after furlough, for those fortunate enough to have been offered this. Even for them, it has meant reduced income, which probably brought with it many intrinsic problems. Hundreds of thousands of people live alone and have suffered from escalating feelings of depression and isolation. The suicide rate has skyrocketed as many, even some of the young, have given up on the future.

We should be aware of the many internal causes of stress, including pessimism, inability to accept uncertainty, not coping with change, rigidity of thought, perfectionism and unrealistic expectations. Some of us make excessive demands on ourselves, use continual negative self-talk and never relax the pressure. Worry is a particularly destructive habit because it wastes energy and tends to focus on the negative, even on the worst-case scenario. As stress builds, any number of health problems start to appear: anxious, racing thoughts; memory, concentration and judgement issues; moodiness, anger, irritability and feelings of overwhelm; aches and pains, rapid heart rate, nausea, diarrhoea, constipation and lack of sex drive.

All forms of stress can be addressed. One of the first things to do is work out the specific causes and consider how they can be mitigated. Even simply talking matters through with a trusted friend, family member or professional is a good starting place. Recognising the symptoms might alert us for the first time that stress is manifesting as an issue in our lives. Sometimes it's just a nagging unexplained pain; for example, in the shoulder or the neck. Usually we recognise a headache as a symptom of pressure and reach for some sort of tablet, but beware: If this becomes a daily habit, it's important to work out the cause of the pressure and take steps to relieve it. Simple daily practices like staying hydrated, breathing deeply whenever we remember, and addressing our sleep environment will help enormously.

As discussed in the section on disease, an improved diet will result in all round better health. Proper nutrition allows us to perform at higher levels. Weight in the right proportion to height places less stress on the body. The average doctor has no time to treat patients holistically, and rarely considers diet during a consultation; the most likely outcome of which is usually some form of chemical remedy. However, if the goal is mind, body and spirit in harmony, then the answers are to be found in relaxation, diet and meditative practices.

We're living at a time unique in history so far. Indeed, there have been other pandemics, and worse diseases which killed off vast numbers of previous populations. But our society has been in a state of chaos and transformation for many years now. Consider the threats from frightening nuclear capabilities, the spectre of global warming (now referred to as climate change), the numerous ongoing wars, ever-growing populations and challenges with producing food; widespread, serious pollution; destruction of the rain forests; the expected financial meltdown; the precarious state of the world economy. The last two, in particular, have been exacerbated by the COVID-19 situation, but perhaps this will prove to be the catalyst for change, the alarm bell that alerts us to the gravity of our circumstances and forces a comprehensive global re-think.

The most significant and achievable influence that we as individuals can have on improving the world situation, is to play our part in raising vibrations globally. Love is the highest vibration, we have been told, but we might wonder what this really means, and ask how we can utilise love to bring about change. The final chapter reflects on love, vibration and hope for the future.

Chapter 10

"All You Need Is Love"

"Love takes up where knowledge leaves off."
St. Thomas Aquinas

Good Vibrations

Looking back over the last century, it seems that we have themes readily identified with most of the decades. The 'teens was the Great War, later known as World War I. Then there was the Roaring Twenties, followed by the depression in the 1930s. It was war again in the 1940s, World War II, and austerity after that right through the 1950s, in the UK at least.

Then came the 1960s with which we associate freedoms of all sorts. Obviously, there was the advent of the pill, but suddenly there was significantly more money coming into circulation, and much of it was in the pockets of the young. It brought a new confidence and feelings of self-assurance and belonging. Popular music became an industry all of its own. When did it start? Was it with Buddy Holly and rock 'n roll at the end of the 1950s? Very regrettably, he died young in a plane crash in 1959, and his life story, as told in the musical *Buddy,* was altogether rather sad. There was none of the wealth enjoyed by later musicians in the industry.

There's something special about numerous tunes of that era, which still play on the radio and over public broadcast systems. The phrase "Summer of Love" kept popping into my mind as I was writing this, and I had an idea that the term is used in connection with 1967; so naturally, I checked up online...

What springs to mind when you hear strains of *Georgy Girl*, an enormously catchy tune performed by **The Seekers,** who were an Australian quartet from Melbourne? I've just learnt that the lyrics were written by **Jim Dale** of *Carry On* fame! Other songs from that summer include *San Francisco, Massachusetts, A Whiter Shade of Pale, Silence is Golden* and numerous numbers by **The Beatles** (1967 was their most prolific year). Most reached the top of the charts, including that used in the title of this chapter, *All You Need is Love.* **The Beach Boys** released *Good Vibrations* in October 1966, but it was still there in the Summer of Love.

Do you feel a rush of nostalgia? Isn't it interesting how music can be so evocative? Incidentally, it seems that some consider 1969 to be the Summer of Love, but 1969 was the summer of Woodstock. What really surprised me, was that there is considered to be a *second* Summer of Love, in 1988! In theory, I should remember this, as I was in the UK at the time, recently qualified as a chartered accountant and settling into a new job with a big firm in Cambridge. I have to say, it passed me by completely—mostly, I recall the music of that time as just noise—for me, it simply didn't have the right vibration.

Reading deeper into the article, I remembered that it was the time of raves, club culture, dance music and ecstasy. I guess this explains everything—it all by-passed me because by then I was working hard on my image as a respectable member of society— or as some might unkindly say, I had already become an apprentice old fogey!

I was watching a webinar recently where the presenter wanted to demonstrate the power of the soundtrack in movie making. The brief clip she used involved a passenger in a taxi, in New York City, who saw his surroundings in quick flashes, as you do in a moving vehicle. When the clip was played for the first time, the music in the background was loud, discordant and a little ominous. All the scenes took on a threatening aspect. Then the identical clip was replayed, with **Pachelbel's** *Canon* as the background track. Suddenly the surroundings looked attractive, friendly and welcoming! Another very clear indication of how vibrations influence our perceptions.

If you aren't familiar with this particular tune, it can easily be found on YouTube. Another wonderful classical experience is the duet from Pearl Fishers, and my preferred version is sung by **Jussi Björling** and **Robert Merrill**. Everyone should have playlists of their favourites for use when they need cheering up, motivation or calming down!

Love, Language and the Subconscious

I can speak only in respect of the English language here, of course, but I suggest that declaring "love" to be an overused word is quite a substantial understatement. That one little word is used to describe so many feelings or states, that it is no surprise that so many have decided that love is nothing but an abstract concept. Or, possibly, they see love in terms only of one of its possible uses, and feel a sense of failure and even inadequacy if that particular form eludes them personally.

I have known for decades that **C S Lewis**, of *Narnia* fame, wrote a book defining love, but I have only recently read it. It is his most well-known non-fiction work, and the title is *The Four Loves.* He bases his distinctions on the four loves defined in the Bible: affection, friendship, erotic love and the love of God. My own view is that the first category, affection, contains a whole raft of sub-categories—including the love mothers have for babies, and indeed all forms of familial love, of which there are many—but the parent-child bond can be incredibly strong; and also in this grouping lie the deep feelings we have for our pets.

In addition, there are the loves we profess to have for foods, sounds, nature, places, experiences, our hobbies, activities and interests. Regarding this list, it could be said that we are using the word in a lazy sense and that with a little effort we could describe our feelings more accurately. But such is language; it's a living thing, and "love" is the word we choose.

Friendship, once seen as enormously important, has been awarded its own category by **Lewis,** but is largely overlooked in society today. Facebook can be said to have devalued the concept, because people collect "friends" like we used to accumulate books, records or CDs, and pay most of them no attention at all. Few would even recognise these "friends" if they happened to turn up at the same function! Many of us refer to people we know only vaguely, as friends, even when, for example, we bump into them only once a year at business meetings. Real friends are to be valued, nurtured and, yes, loved.

Romantic love is often conflated with passion, and when the emotion dulls over time, it can be thought that love has gone. Sometimes this is where friendship steps into the breach, or a form of deep affection replaces the initial ardour. According to **Lewis**, the Bible says that the bond between a man and a woman represents God's love for the world, but he also defines it as charity, or "agape." He says that the other three forms of love can be considered a training ground for this category. He not only calls this unconditional love, but also describes it as love for our fellow man and even love for ourselves.

Most of us will be familiar with the parable of the Good Samaritan, as told in **Matthew,** and also perhaps with the instruction that one should "Love thy neighbour as thyself." Yet what is often overlooked here, is the instruction that we should love ourselves: So many of us feel that this is somehow wrong, selfish or self-indulgent. Countless negative beliefs and programs have been instilled since childhood, and frequently we are not even aware of them. This often results in our being very hard on ourselves as a sort of default position.

Held deep in the subconscious are memories of which we have no active recollection, which nevertheless have a deep effect on our everyday lives. Those struggling to find love, or lasting relationships, could find that they have trouble *giving* love because they don't even love themselves. Others hold a feeling of unworthiness, and find it difficult to *receive* love. Simply recognising that this could be an issue is a great first step towards building a better and more fulfilled life.

Love Changes Everything

"Love changes everything," sang **Michael Ball** in 1992, from the musical *Aspects of Love.* Strangely, I had remembered the song title as "Love Conquers Everything," but I guess the sentiment is more or less the same. It is an indisputable truth.

In 1969 the musical *Goodbye Mr Chips* was released, starring **Peter O'Toole** and **Petula Clarke.** Most of its tunes are long forgotten, but one seemed to resonate with everybody: the school song, entitled *Fill the World With Love.* My brother's secondary school opened the doors to its first pupils a few years later, and in due course a vote was held in conjunction with a competition to compose a suitable school song. The decision was made to adopt *Fill the World With Love.* To many this seemed a little over sentimental, almost a form of cheating; but now all of us participate in the nostalgia intended by the writers. It was the perfect choice – great words and such evocative vibrations!

Love is part of the storyline of nearly every movie. How many of the great epics spring to mind, before you remember one where love wasn't involved? They exist, of course, but it seems that producers feel that there has to be at least some sort of love interest within the plot to keep the audience engaged, and usually this will be romantic love. One of the all-time best "feel good movies" might be *Love Actually,* which is a beautiful mix of eight different love stories, not all of them what you might call typical.

Love has been called the "universal solvent." Nothing can withstand the presence of love. It is the highest of vibrations, and everything responds to it. Imagine if everyone radiated love, what the effect on the universal field would be. There simply could not be any war. An experiment was carried out where a group of about thirty meditators focused on peace, love and harmony for a month, and the crime rate reported in that city for the same period was reduced by more than 50%.

We are aware that knowledge and technology was astonishingly advanced in ancient Egypt, many millennia ago. I have referred, in Chapters 1 and 4, to man's considerable latent powers and the theories held by sages that we might have destroyed ourselves several times over in past civilizations. Deep in the chakras, specifically chakra 2, there are powers that are withheld from us in our current state of development. Apparently, the Egyptians became aware that they were overreaching themselves, that they had become too advanced in their knowledge and were accessing powers that were destructive, frightening and uncontrollable. They contacted the Hathors, extra-terrestrial beings who have been described as our elder brothers and sisters in consciousness. They are masters of sound and energy and have been involved in the development of humans on Earth for millennia.

During the Egyptian era, they worked through the sky deity Hathor, and used the Pyramid of Balance to expand consciousness to a maximum level. They claim that a state of "universal androgyny" will be reached once the so-called male and female flows are in balance—this will open the gate to the deeper mysteries of our own consciousness. The energy they used to rectify the Egyptian situation was pure love, and certain individuals even today are engaged in spreading the messages of the Hathors, along with their advanced practices.

Unconditional Love

Although we are told that God's love for us in unconditional, there are many for whom this statement will have little meaning, because not all of us have experienced unconditional love. I would describe it as the love that mothers—and fathers— receive from their babies as they develop from helpless bundles and become individual little people. Usually, the same love is reciprocated, but when this is not the case, as can happen for a multitude of reasons, the effect on the unloved person is profound. Humans need love. And this deep affection, with no strings attached, is the highest form of love. Parents usually maintain this unconditional love for their offspring right through to adulthood and often beyond, even though there could be a complete absence of "like" in the teenage years.

The knowledge that they are loved, for its own sake and with no reciprocation expected, is the most solid of foundations that we can give our children. We want them to grow in confidence and leave the nest when ready, feeling worthy and comfortable in their own skin.

As they grow and explore romantic relationships, those who succeed best in this critical part of life are those who can both give and receive love. We have to feel worthy of love before we are truly able to receive it. Truly loving means wanting the best for the other person, as opposed to "what can this person give me in this relationship?" Too many relationships flounder because they are built on a subconscious, materialistic foundation.

Those of us who have known the love of a pet—past or present—will have felt the warmth and power of unconditional love. I've been fortunate to have owned numerous cats, as well as a few lovely dogs, and I'll argue with anyone that cats can indeed give plenty of love, although as a species they have the reputation of being aloof and self-contained. My husband would tell me that the love I received from my cats was cupboard love, because they knew where their next meal was coming from. I begged to differ! But with dogs, there is no argument. They accept you as boss; you are their world, and they give one hundred percent devotion.

Not only should we aspire to love ourselves, but we should do so unconditionally. This is emphatically not selfish, albeit we have probably all been told when growing up that this is the case. It might even account for the fact that most of us are our own worst critics, often without realising it. We are dissatisfied with our appearances, particularly with parts of it that we think we can improve, such as our weight or fitness level. We undergo continual punishing routines of diet and exercise, and blame ourselves when we "fail" to achieve the desired results.

You know that nagging little voice that lives within all our heads? How quickly it's ready to criticise when we commit even the most trifling act of forgetfulness, clumsiness or similar? What derogatory names do you call yourself on a daily basis? Idiot, twit, BF or fool? No, probably much, much worse than that, with a four-letter adjective in front! And generally for no good reason—it's just a reflex and we all do it.

Cease the negative self-talk! The all-powerful subconscious is what hears these insults, and they have the same effect as berating a young child over and over again for the mildest of misbehaviours or accidents. If a child grows up receiving nothing but abuse, we know what the results will be. And importantly, that child will learn to be afraid of showing initiative or making decisions. So notice how often you criticise yourself without thinking! Stop yourself and say, "Cancel, cancel, no big deal," or whatever works for you. More importantly, develop a new habit: When you get things right, acknowledge it. Say, "Well done!" "Top of the Class," or something similar.

Intentions, Life Purpose and Soul Purpose

It will soon be a century since **Napoleon Hill** published *Think and Grow Rich*, one of the earliest books on personal development (PD). The research for that book involved 20 years of work! Others have taken up the mantle and, particularly since the rise of the internet, it seems that the majority of people have had at least some exposure to PD. When I was working full time, I was encouraged to access some professional development training, but little emphasis was placed on PD, which was usually referred to as the "soft skills." Out of interest, I read various "self-help" books, as they were labelled until quite recently, but it's only since I quit the rat race that I've had time to study psychology, philosophy and theology in any depth.

When we dabble in subjects, and we don't or can't get really invested in them, no visible results will appear. This is why we are encouraged to set goals, or targets, because in so doing we can measure our gains or at least register where our attention still needs to be focused. It's important to consider the intention behind the focus or the target. For example, the goal might be to pass an exam—but why? Is the exam the "end goal" or the "means goal?"

The intention could be to qualify in a profession, or to obtain a certification so that more money may be earned. Intentions are what drive us and cause us to choose what we do. Knowing the intention behind our actions allows us to fine-tune our activity. Goals are more likely to be achieved when the thought process behind setting them is conscious and aligned with our values. So when setting a goal, to ensure we have chosen the right one, we are advised to ask "why," and for each answer, ask "why" again (up to seven times). This technique allows us to identify what is really driving our actions.

Thanks largely to advances in technology and, of course, to the internet, the amount of in-depth knowledge and PD readily available now, via courses, books, webinars, YouTube and so on—often free or at really low cost—is nothing short of mind-blowing. Young people might take this for granted but nevertheless have exposure to amazing opportunities, of which the majority of the population used to live in ignorance. In addition, ready and willing to take advantage, there's a veritable army of vibrant, enthusiastic folk who have maybe come to the end of their working lives by choice, or finished raising their families, and want to occupy their minds whilst achieving something useful with their newfound free time.

There are still others who have been made redundant or similar at an unacceptably young age and find themselves seeking some kind of income-generating work—it never used to be a concern that people would outlive their savings. The result is a vast number of experienced people, of many different ages and levels of education, seeking and gaining knowledge which almost invariably includes some level of PD. A significant amount of PD overlaps with spirituality, which in due course causes them to ponder questions such as, "How can I contribute?" "How can I give back?" and even, "What is the purpose of this (or my) life?"

We find ourselves at a stage in society's evolution like never before, where so many have the time, money and inclination to reflect on whether they can improve the quality and direction of not only their lives but the lives of others as well. Perhaps this goes towards explaining the global awakening that is undoubtedly occurring. It will serve everyone, even those who have no idea that it is happening.

Yet this awakening is progressing at a time of unbelievable challenge. The COVID-19 pandemic, which entered our reality early in 2020, has totally disrupted life as we knew it, and we recognise that things will never be the same again. It's regrettable that for the first 9 months or so, a majority of the PD gurus were simply ignoring the dramatic effect that the virus was having on so many lives, in terms of the economy, income and uncertainty about the future. Perhaps they saw it as a short-term interruption, easily solved (for them) by presenting online instead of in person at a venue.

I wonder if they imagined that by ignoring the COVID-19 situation, it might go away! Their course content didn't change, and most of the Americans didn't even drop their prices—Tony Robbins being a notable exception (at least for Unleash the Power Within). No wonder many reported their best year ever—suddenly they had a huge worldwide audience, with no rental fees to pay for venues—yet still they had no advice for those struggling with the new paradigm. When occasionally an attendee asked about it during a live Q & A session, they were usually berated for negative thinking!

So, if we operate from the position that everything is happening for the best, and that we actively chose to be here in these incomprehensible times... how do we get to see the full picture? The world is in a state of great upheaval, but there has to be an upturn, and it will happen when we are ready for it—when the stage is set. It's a matter of timing: Divine Right Timing.

Referring back to Chapter 7, I mentioned the concept of soul purpose. To distinguish your soul purpose from your life purpose, the first may be considered spiritual and esoteric— possibly the subject matter for a whole lecture, or even a book.

The second is physical—something we choose or recognise in this lifetime. Many go through life without identifying either, but those fortunate enough to reach the top of the Maslow pyramid, will find that they feel something is missing in their lives if they have no purpose. Younger people, fully engaged in raising families, climbing the career ladder and often struggling with overwhelm, probably give this rather important aspect of life no thought at all; or, if asked, would consider that they were busy pursuing it. It's usually when we are in the third stage of life, with time to call our own, that we have the knowledge, awareness and inclination to identify our life purpose.

Energy, Consciousness and Love

The heart is the access point to our inner selves, and it's in constant communication with the brain. We have a spiritual heart and a physical heart. The voice of the heart is intuition, which can propel us to move beyond our limitations. We know that our emotions can renew or drain us, and as we learn to manage the signals that our hearts are sending, we can upscale the quality of our lives. Appreciation is a quality of the heart, along with compassion, gratitude, care, kindness, patience and most importantly, love. Other, less frequently discussed heart emotions are nobility, honour, dignity and courage, which reflect the higher levels of our nature. When we manifest these qualities, life will treat us differently. It's essential that we reconnect with our hearts, and remember that we are all connected to one another.

At this landmark time in our history, as life seems to fly past ever faster, we find that more and more is expected of us. Our frames of reference are constantly changing, which can have a truly unsettling effect. As a result, many are facing exhaustion, overwhelm or loneliness. Technology has potentially made us more connected than ever before, yet feelings of isolation and rejection are widespread. The COVID-19 pandemic may be seen as a wake-up call, ordering us to examine what's wrong with the way we live, the food we eat and the way we treat other living beings. If it is an impetus for positive change, then good will result from it. Together we have the ability to use this experience as an empowerment opportunity.

The hippie movement, in the 1960s, famously urged us just to love one another, so that all our problems would be solved. At the time, powerful hallucinogenic drugs were unregulated and in common use, and the hippie message became inextricably mingled with excessive freedom, promiscuity, and irresponsibility. So the memory and the message have been distorted, with little positive remaining—but what if the love they were talking about was not romantic love but unconditional love?

Their philosophy was revived to an extent by so-called New Age thinking, which arose around 1970, and the label is still used to describe practices that are largely spiritual and definitely outside of organised religion. It seems now to have been bracketed with the New World Order, seen these days as Orwellian but originally anticipated by New Agers as a sort of utopia under the charge of a (benevolent) world government, and comprising absence of disease, hunger, pollution and poverty.

The awakening that is underway now, results from more and more motivated people seeking answers to the chaos and confusion surrounding us. The dreaded virus has only magnified existing perceptions that the world we live in could be spiralling out of control, in themselves leading to loss of emotional equilibrium. But we are aware of numerous techniques for dealing with inflammatory situations and re-establishing calm.

Mindfulness, meditation and yoga are at the top of the list. We know that we have been misled, poorly educated and are still being misinformed. However, knowledge is power, so long as the knowledge is applied to good effect. Science and spirituality are aligning with increasing speed as we learn more about the Divine Matrix which connects us all.

We are told that what we appreciate, appreciates, and that what we resist, persists. We understand the importance of vibration, and even how to access the powers of our higher selves. We're aware that we have three brains, and that what we know as intuition can be nurtured and magnified as we learn to look out for signals from the body. We know about the health benefits of proper breathing, nutrition, hydration, and management of sleep and stress.

We recognise the importance of love, in all its many forms, but specifically that unconditional love is love manifesting in its highest form. With the mind, body and spirit fully connected, we find ourselves operating in a virtual cycle of physical and psychological coherence, where anything is possible in a glorious setting of synchronicity and serendipity. We are spirit and are coming into our power. This is the great awakening, in which everyone, without exception, is invited to participate.

About the Author

Anne Corbin grew up in southern Africa, has travelled widely, worked in 3 continents, and visited all of them! Now firmly based in the UK, she hopes that opportunities for travel will resume shortly.

Having obtained a BSc, then a PGCE, Anne taught mathematics and science for several years. Next, preferring to work in the "real world," she qualified as a chartered accountant, practised professionally for 12 years, and worked in business for 10. Anne became one of the pioneers promoting the importance of the work-life balance, and after quitting the rat race, spent several years offering private tuition, whilst indulging her passion for exploring exotic locations.

Anne has lectured at conferences and contributed to training manuals, whilst sitting on numerous panels and committees, both business and environmental. She is a volunteer crew-member with the Tall Ships Youth Trust, and participates (when possible) in an annual voyage on a tall ship, working as the purser/medic.

Whilst continuing to invest in her own personal development, Anne recognises the benefits of having multiple income streams, and strongly believes that we should never stop learning. She invests in property, is an independent consultant for Arbonne

International and actively promotes the principles of the Energy Codes™ through coaching and lecturing, having achieved certification through The Morter Institute. Anne can be contacted via anne@annecorbin.com

Anne enjoys life in rural Cambridgeshire, where her hobbies include reading, cooking, theatre, cinema, and history. Her previous two books are available from Amazon, using the links provided below:

Property Investing 2020 and Beyond
Amazon.com - http://tiny.cc/acrealestatebook
Amazon.co.uk - http://tiny.cc/acpropertybook

The Authorities : Everything Is Energy
Amazon.com - http://tiny.cc/authoritiesUSA
Amazon.co.uk - http://tiny.cc/authorities

Anne's podcast,
The Mind-Body-Spirit Connection
is available on all the usual platforms.

Her training can be found on awaken.plus
and you can schedule a call with Anne
with this link: calendly.com/mbsconnect

Printed in Great Britain
by Amazon

80890448R10108